Stock Market Stratagem

Loss Control and Portfolio Management Enhancement

Braden Glett

Senior Partner of Business Diagnosis and Improvement, Inc.

THOMSON
™

Australia · Canada · Mexico · Singapore · Spain · United Kingdom · United States

THOMSON

™

STOCK MARKET STRATAGEM: LOSS CONTROL AND PORTFOLIO MANAGEMENT ENHANCEMENT
Braden Glett

Editor-in-Chief:
Jack Calhoun

**Vice President/
Executive Publisher:**
Dave Shaut

Acquisitions Editor:
Steve Momper

**Channel Manager,
Retail:**
Bari Shokler

**Channel Manager,
Professional:**
Mark Linton

Production Editor:
Alan Biondi

Production Manager:
Tricia Matthews Boies

**Manufacturing
Coordinator:**
Charlene Taylor

Compositor:
Edgewater Editorial
Services

Editorial Associate:
Michael Jeffers

Production Associate:
Barbara Evans

Printer:
Edwards Brothers, Inc.
Ann Arbor, MI

Cover Designer:
Chris A. Miller

TABLE OF CONTENTS

About the Author

Braden Glett is the founder of Business Diagnosis & Improvement, a consulting firm specializing in general management and profitability improvement for manufacturing-based businesses.

Mr. Glett has close to 20 years of experience in strategic development, financial management, marketing management, market research, and operations. Highly creative and analytical, he is particularly expert in systematic processes for identifying policy-based and operations-based constraints on profitability and in crafting countermeasures to remove those constraints. He also excels in integrating financial measures and internal processes to reduce such constraints. Among his other strengths are creativity in combining disciplines to solve entrenched business problems.

He has started and aggressively expanded several businesses and has helped run businesses varying in size from $1MM to $500MM in annual sales. Expert in understanding financial markets and investment principles, he has successfully managed his own portfolio for more than two decades.

Mr. Glett received a joint M.B.A. and B.S.B.A. in finance from Bowling Green State University in Ohio.

LIST OF FIGURES

LIST OF TABLES

INTRODUCTION

This is a book about how to pick a portfolio of winning stocks, and about how to manage that portfolio to increase your odds of achieving excellent results. By the time you have finished reading this book, you will know exactly how to find high-potential stocks, when to buy, when to add to a position, when to sell, and how to control your risk throughout.

Today most books about the stock market, including those for the experienced or professional investor, concern themselves almost exclusively with selecting stocks; any details about how to manage the risks associated with investing are very sketchy. These books largely neglect the most critical aspect of investing—loss control—and its necessary adjunct—portfolio management.

Recent bearish action in the stock market has painfully highlighted for many investors the need for something more, a structure for avoiding loss of principal that also offers opportunities for incredible upside growth. Most investors have no well-founded concepts, no specific plans, no tools for controlling risk, and no understanding of the need to manage their portfolios. They therefore tend to be driven by their emotions, oscillating between excessively concentrated portfolios (generally culminating at the market's top) and excessively conservative portfolios (at the bottom).

The lack of a comprehensive algorithm for portfolio control (and hence, risk control) often results in perfectly wrong timing of these two extremes. There is simply a dearth of useful literature on capital preservation and portfolio management. This book aims to fill that gap. It will give serious equity investors an unambiguous methodology for being in the right stocks, at the right time, in the right proportions, and with the right exit system. Hence, a large part of this book is concerned with minimizing losses as a means of reaping gains—the gains that inevitably come over time to holders of growth stocks.

The current, inadequate books on investing generally include highly subjective and complex laundry lists of loss-cutting rules, sell signals, rules of thumb for buying, et cetera, that are impossible to implement objectively. Many of the rules conflict with each other, which further adds to the confusion. What these books do not provide is help on how much of each stock to buy, when to sell specific stocks, when to add to or subtract from positions, when to stop adding to positions, and where to place stop orders.

Particularly neglected are the subjects of how much to invest in each stock, and when and how to exit profitable positions. While these subjects are given lip service in nearly every book, they are not addressed in a clear, comprehensive, or unambiguous way. Up until now it has been mostly left to individual readers to create their own systems for managing their portfolios—a costly exercise in terms of time and mistakes made.

This book will give you the airtight portfolio methodology you need to control losses. It explores in detail some common scenarios and the fallacies that lead to the majority of stock market losses. Our examination of mistakes leads to a straightforward set of portfolio management rules—the Reverse Scale System introduced in Chapter 10.

Since a stock that fails to advance at least in step with the market can be considered a loss for all practical purposes, how to pick high-potential stocks is a critical aspect of the book. By analyzing the selection mistakes that account for the majority of investor losses, we come to a set of selection criteria that, while simple, are powerful and will effectively steer your portfolio toward big winners.

Given recent market conditions, a hot-button subject for most investors is how to integrate market conditions into a portfolio system. A simple yet effective way to essentially turn off stock selection until conditions improve is presented in Chapter 12. It reduces the potential for excessive whipsaw losses—a significant threat in a downtrending market.

A word to the wise: Do-it-yourself investing can be costly if you do not have the discipline or interest to learn and apply all the rules and techniques provided between these two covers. The good news is that if you do have the discipline, systematic portfolio management can be an extremely rewarding, even life-changing, pursuit.

SECTION I
FOUNDATIONAL CONCEPTS

CHAPTER 1

THE CASE FOR AN ACTIVELY MANAGED PORTFOLIO

In this chapter I would like to convince you that at least some portion of your assets should be in an actively managed portfolio of individual stocks—and not just mindlessly indexed to some market average, as is all the rage now. Though throughout this chapter I may seem to be predicting changes in the market environment, I am not. I am only trying to expand your thinking about the range of possible future market conditions, because as investors we need to consider all contingencies. We cannot blindly assume that the situation will remain static—or even consistent with recent history. If we do, we run the risk of not being prepared for plausible scenarios; that preparation is essential if we are concerned with loss control.

A BRIEF REVIEW OF THE TWENTIETH CENTURY

The passing of generations erases the collective memory. That is why the popular perception of market returns today is colored exclusively by the memory of market returns in the last half of the twentieth century. Because so many people boast these days about being long-term investors, let us take a truly long-term view and consider what the term "long-term investor" may actually mean.

The first 40 years of the twentieth century were not so kind to equity investors as the latter part of the century was. The Dow Jones Industrial Average (DJIA), which started the century at 68.13, first achieved the

3

lofty level of 100 on January 12, 1906.[1] The average traded below 100 at some point in each of the following years all the way through 1925, five times in the 1930s, and for the last time in 1942.

If there had been such funds then, anyone investing in a DJIA index fund in January 1906 would have collected nothing but dividends (no capital gains, in other words) as late as 1942, a period of about 36 years. Given current sky-high valuations on the stocks represented in today's index funds, could that happen again? Some say no, because results in the first 40 years of the twentieth century were influenced by at least one World War (1917-18) and by part of another. Are we now immune from the possibility of war, and its effects? Others say no, another long dry period could not happen because we now have great technological advances. Yet in some ways, the technology advances of 1906 to 1942, relatively speaking, may have been even greater than today's: Americans went from horse travel and medicine shows to X-rays, penicillin, radio, and early jet aircraft.

Each period in history is unique and unpredictable, yet it would be difficult to explain why economic history *cannot* repeat itself. We must not let our optimism about the future cause us to jump to the conclusion that passive investing will reap gigantic (or even respectable) returns in every 10-year period—especially when history shows us otherwise. In any case, as investors it ought not to be our aim to predict anything but to plan for a full range of possible scenarios.

On the positive side, and contrary to popular belief, though the bull market of 1982 through 1999 was unusual, it was not totally unprecedented. The DJIA shows a 24-year super-bull market from 1942 through 1966; it was during this period that the Dow leaped up from 100 to 1,000; the 1982-1999 market raised the Dow tenfold, from under 1,000 to over 10,000, in only 18 years. Obviously, the annualized rate of return between 1982 and 1999 was also far higher, but the extraordinary thing about the 1982-1999 period in the United States was not the rate of return but the sustained, very high, valuations relative to earnings of the largest stocks in the major indexes. We are still waiting to see how this situation will finally resolve itself, whether in an extraordinary growth in future earnings of these large companies (entirely possible) or a long period of

---

[1]Phyllis S. Pierce, ed. *The Dow-Jones Averages 1885-1985.* Homewood, IL: Dow-Jones Irwin, 1986.

under-performance while earnings gradually catch up (also entirely possible). Everyone hopes for the former, but we must prepare for the latter, allowing for both cases in our investment philosophy.

It is *de rigueur* in the financial services industry to repeat the mantra that stocks return 9 percent per year in the long run. The long run is then often underestimated as being five to 10 years. As investors thinking for ourselves, we need to recognize that a comparison of the very long-term with returns of 9 percent with the substantially greater returns of the past 20 years may suggest the recurrence of a period of muted returns like that of 1966 through 1982 (there were similar periods in 1835 through 1860 and 1906 through 1942 as well).

The lesson is this:

The long run can be very long for the passive investor in an average stock. The key question for every investor is therefore: Can you afford to place all of the growth portion of your portfolio for the next 10 years into a basket that mindlessly accepts the average market return, when that average return may be insufficient to provide for your needs?

If not, you'd better not rely on index funds alone for all your investment returns. Consider using some portion of your funds to seek out growth opportunities in exceptional individual stocks.

Although the two super-bull markets of 1942 to 1966 and 1982 to 1999 could repeat themselves, it is not a given that this will happen. A period of index underperformance (underperformance relative to reasonable investor expectations), most likely manifesting itself as a long-lasting limited trading range, is possible, and an objective person planning for retirement or other future needs must allow for it. Nevertheless, though speculation about the future direction of the stock market is futile, the assumption that the "average investor" will be satisfied with the returns on an "average stock" is a valid question.

THERE IS ALMOST ALWAYS SOMETHING DOING WELL

By investing in the averages, you cannot possibly avoid average results. The really good news, though, is that while market averages may possibly dawdle for some time, there are always some companies going up far above the average. This is the allure of the actively managed portfolio. By highly selective investing in individual stocks, you have a good chance of staying ahead of the averages. Using the criteria presented in Section II,

Stock Selection, will improve those chances. Keeping in mind the possibilities for long, dry periods for the average stock, wouldn't you like to find some of the stellar performers?

Despite the bear market prevailing in 2000-2002,[2] among 7,800 of the most actively-traded stocks, a number of stocks at least doubled in value during the period (see Table 1-1).

TABLE 1-1: STOCKS THAT MORE THAN DOUBLED IN VALUE

Two-Year Returns of:	Number of Stocks
900 percent or more	7
700 percent to 899 percent	5
400 percent to 499 percent	53
300 percent to 399 percent	49
200 percent to 299 percent	155
100 percent to 199 percent	573
Total	**842**

This period included the worst bear market in at least 18 years; the price of the average stock as measured by the S&P 500 index fell by about 18 percent,[2] and other market indexes fell much more. The point of this table is not that you should be investing aggressively during bear markets—you shouldn't, and how to avoid this is addressed later. But spending the time to identify stocks that will perform better than average can be highly profitable if you have real money to invest. (During a bull market, of course, the number of stocks more than doubling is substantially higher than in bear markets, so that is when you really want to be looking for doublers.)

With 842 stocks that more than doubled over a two-year bear market period, you probably would have enough stocks to choose from for your personal portfolio. You only need 10 or 20. But, you ask, could we have found the stocks that performed well *before* they had exhausted their run? We could (and I did find some of them during this period), for one simple reason: *These moves don't all happen in one day.* It's not as though we see a $10 stock, wake up the next day and—Eureka!—suddenly, the stock

---

[2]April 19, 2000 to April 18, 2002.

is now trading at $50. Such moves take time, and stocks that are in the ascension process make new highs with some regularity all the while. Later, I encourage you to increase your odds of finding ascending stocks by looking only at stocks that are making new price highs for the year. There are other criteria, of course, but the fact that a stock is near its high for the year substantially increases its odds of giving a good return.

In addition to the ever-present rewards of investing in individual stocks, there may be other timely reasons why this is a good idea. Among them:

1. The growth of index funds has driven many investors into the same set of large-capitalization stocks. In the equities markets, mechanically doing what the herd is doing seldom yields great results.

2. Demographic trends that supported the bull market of the past twenty years will be shifting in the coming decade.

INDEX FUNDS: A POTENTIAL SOURCE OF UNDERPERFORMANCE

Index funds are mutual funds that mirror the performance of major stock indexes. They came into being in reaction to the poor performance of certain nonindexed mutual funds, as a way to practically guarantee investors that their funds would not under perform the market averages. Not only do they offer this guarantee but usually they also sport very low annual maintenance expenses. Hence, their popularity, the amount of money invested in indexed mutual funds has grown tremendously over the past 10 years.

Indexing has somewhat artificially funneled tremendous amounts of money into the very largest companies in the market. The inflow of funds into index funds may be one of the reasons why we currently see such tremendous differences in valuations between the largest-capitalization and the smallest-capitalization companies.

Index funds are those that track the S&P 500. The S&P 500 itself is a capitalization-weighted index. Hence, S&P 500 index mutual funds must pour heavy amounts of their cash into the companies that have the highest market capitalization in order to ensure that their performance will mirror the index's. This, of course, further raises the market value of the firms indexed and gives them even more weight in the index, and the cycle continues.

Granted, even before the advent of index funds, mutual fund managers faced tremendous temptation to own the very largest, most popular companies. However, if the price of those companies got too far out of line with their actual values, the manager was free to sell them. This is not generally true with index funds. Index fund managers must buy the companies represented in the index, without regard to the relationship of share cost to value or the future earnings potential of the companies, in other words, no matter how absurd the valuation. Couple this with the fact that these funds represent one of the largest, most popular current investment vehicles and you can see how, over time, lots of money ends up chasing very few stocks.

How much of current valuation issues are related to this? How will this situation defuse itself? We really don't know. The distortion in value of S&P 500 companies does not seem to be nearly as great as the value distortion during the dot-com bubble of the late 1990s. On the other hand, the sheer number of dollars involved potentially represents a far greater misallocation of capital. It may also spell minuscule returns on these largest companies even while underlying earnings advance. Again, this is not inevitable; it's just a possible outcome to plan for. While it is obviously impossible for an S&P 500 index fund to under perform the S&P 500 itself, it may well be that the index itself will not deliver returns in line with reasonable investor needs and expectations.

Wall Street has chased a few anointed stocks many other times before. In 1972, *Institutional Investor* singled out 17 growth stocks that had perfect financials and fundamental characteristics: American Home Products, Avon Products, Coca-Cola, Walt Disney, Eastman Kodak, IBM, AT&T, Johnson & Johnson, S.S. Kresge, Eli Lilly, McDonald's, Merck, MGIC Investment, 3M, Polaroid, Sears, and Xerox. Ten years later, the group of stocks still had not returned to even break-even performance for their shareholders.[3] Although some of them have since gone on to spectacular gains, it was a long, long wait for investors who followed the herd and bought these "must-own" stocks in 1972. The outlook for buyers of

---

[3]Norman G. Fosback, *Stock Market Logic.* Washington, D.C.: Institute for Econometric Research, 18th printing, 1990), pp. 325-26.

"must-own" stocks in *any* other time frame is probably very similar. Emulating the crowd is not a behavior highly rewarded on Wall Street.

A market scenario of winners and losers, or a two-tiered market, argues strongly for the value of highly selective stock picking and active management. Besides, whether times are good or bad, the potential gains from an *actively* and *correctly* managed portfolio of high-potential stocks are always greater than the gains possible by simply throwing money into an indexed mutual fund.

Though speculation about the future is futile, we can at least hazard a guess that the continuance in 2002 of extremely high valuation in the largest-capitalization stocks may argue for us to de-emphasize passive investment approaches and re-emphasize the basic disciplines of active investment.

DEMOGRAPHIC SHIFTS

Unfolding demographic shifts in the U.S. population may also argue for rifle-shot rather than shotgun investment approaches. As the baby-boom postwar generation has been saving for retirement they have brought large inflows of capital into the stock and bond markets, which will begin to be drawn away as this generation retires. It seems likely that with-drawals may start to outweigh inflows possibly starting in about 2006 through 2010. Because the baby boomer generation generally had small-er families than previous generations, it is not a given that inflows from the retirement savings of their children will offset the outflows caused by boomer post-retirement withdrawals. These outflows may depress returns somewhat, although no one knows to what degree.

The large demographic-based 1982-2000 inflows into S&P 500 index funds may have contributed to some of the huge differences in valuations between the highest-capitalization companies and those not heavily rep-resented in the indexes. Because this hypothesis cannot be proven, think of it only as a possibility, not a certainty. Nevertheless, the hypothesis has enough credibility to warrant incorporating it into our possible investment scenarios. The shift from inflows to net outflows may slowly let the air out of these mega-cap stocks in the coming decade. Though anything can happen, it would seem prudent to be aware of this and use some funds to pursue high-performance, relatively unknown stocks as the coming decade unfolds, rather than just chasing the largest, highest-profile stocks that everyone is watching.

WHY YOU CAN BEAT THE PERFORMANCE OF MOST MUTUAL FUNDS

Individual investors have only one concern, and that is, of course, to make as much money as possible, as quickly as possible. Mutual fund managers, on the other hand, have to balance many conflicting goals. They cannot be concerned with results alone. One thing they must be able to do is to justify why they bought a stock, especially if that stock does poorly enough to affect results. Since any major position can potentially affect results negatively, they must therefore be able to show that just about every stock appeared to be unquestionably good when they bought it.

If their bosses happen to be big believers in financial ratios, fund managers will need to make sure the ratios of most things they buy are reasonable—whether or not that actually matters. Since they will probably not be able to change a boss's deep-seated belief that ratio analysis is a good predictor of results, most of them will "get with the program." Otherwise, it may appear they did not do a good due diligence job, a process that should concern itself primarily with validating each company's value proposition, management competence, and solvency.

This is one reason why most mutual funds are attracted to large-cap stocks with picture-perfect earnings trends and financial ratios, even at the expense of return (little risk, little return). This is in fact one reason that many mutual funds under perform—and why an individual like you can outperform them.

An individual also has the advantage of being able to buy and sell small positions with relative ease, to cut a loss or lock in a profit when the trend has clearly turned.

As an individual investor, you have many advantages that allow you to concentrate on discovering what works and how to apply it. Some of these are:

1. You'll never be asked why you had a bad quarter, so that you can ride longer trends with some downs as well as ups along the way.

2. You'll never need to dress up your portfolio at the end of the quarter so that it's shown holding the most recent glamour stocks.

3. You'll never have to explain to a committee why you bought a stock that ended up with a loss.

4. Unless you have a very large amount of money, you'll probably never have to spend hours or days trying to slowly unwind a large position that is declining.

5. You can truly diversify, rather than diversifying around the fringes of "core holdings" that include the must-own darlings that are also held by most other mutual funds.

6. If a position grows to more than 5 percent of your portfolio, you won't have to trim it to satisfy regulatory requirements.

Of course, you will have to suffer the results of mistakes you make, and they may be big ones if you don't work to truly understand the difference between the investment principles that are common "wisdom" and those that actually work in the real world.

CHAPTER SUMMARY

We should not confuse an optimistic outlook for the future with the idea that the future will be equally bright for all investments, or for investors who mindlessly do what everyone else is doing. The return for the *average* stock, especially the average high-cap stock, could be a lot lower going forward than it has been in recent years—as has been true during some long periods in the past. Beating the market indexes may be necessary to satisfy your need for strong returns.

The good news is there are always stocks that are doing far better than the averages. It makes sense, for those people so inclined, to add an actively managed portfolio of select individual stocks to their broad investment plan.

The good news is also this: No matter what the future may hold for the general market, the rewards of investing in individual stocks are substantial. If you use the criteria for picking stocks I present in this book, you will greatly increase your odds of finding above-average stocks—and getting above-market returns.

CHAPTER 2
ASSET ALLOCATION FOR THE 21ST CENTURY

TYPES OF FINANCIAL INVESTMENTS

Before we launch into the exciting subject of how to become a success in the stock market, let's take a step back and go through the discipline of thinking about your entire financial picture. No doubt you have some financial investments already, or you would not be reading this book. Although this is not a book about financial planning generally, it *is* a book about your financial survival, and nothing is more important to your financial survival than understanding where your true risks lie. Only by surviving the short-term financial hurdles of life can we realize the long-term rewards of investing.

Most of our investments can be categorized as either contingent or noncontingent investments.

Contingent investments are those that are dependent on some unpredictable event; they include life, disability, healthcare, long-term care, auto, and homeowners' insurance. Because these investments are by their nature oriented toward loss control (e.g., the loss of your income or your health or your home), they are therefore very important. Any book on loss control (and loss control is an integral part of this one) would be incomplete without at least mentioning the need for these types of investments.

Especially if you have dependents, make your contingent investments before you even think about investing in stocks. Although that advice may seem obvious, you probably know from experience that many people ignore it completely. The risk of losing money in stocks is generally paltry compared to the losses you can incur by ignoring contingent investments. I recently read that the average court award in civil lawsuits is now several hundred thousand dollars, but even that much loss is small compared to the incalculable suffering your dependents would experience if you were killed or rendered unable to work. That's why disability and life insurance are just as important as the liability insurance you carry on your car. You certainly are worth more than your car, or any damage it can cause. Do your contingent investments reflect that fact?

Noncontingent investments are those that have value in and of themselves, independent of any event. They include our homes, stocks, bonds, bank accounts, and practically everything else we own. Each category has its own characteristics and each has different keys to success: the keys to succeeding in real estate investing are far different than the keys to succeed in investing in stocks.

This book will show you exactly how to avoid losses in stocks and come out a winner. In fact, 90 percent of the subject matter between these two covers is related strictly to stock investments. But first let's discuss how you might structure your entire portfolio of noncontingent financial investments (stocks and all other financial assets) to survive through almost any economic scenario you might confront. Having a balanced portfolio can give you peace of mind, giving you a better chance of holding on to stocks that are trending upward even with temporary corrections in price. The ability to hold on during corrections is necessary if you are to achieve large capital gains; having a diversity of asset classes beyond stocks and cash can help to smooth the ride and contain emotionally-based buying and selling.

SOME BASIC THOUGHTS ON ASSET ALLOCATION AND PORTFOLIO DIVERSIFICATION

The best defense against general economic distress is to keep your portfolio balanced at all times. If you take care of the risks in your portfolio, to a large extent the profits will take care of themselves. While most people understand this intuitively, there is a lot of fuzzy thinking sloshing around on the subject of just what a diversified portfolio is. Let's talk about it briefly just to make sure your financial foundation is secure and that all the bases are covered. Once you get some serious money in your investment portfolio, it pays to take a good hard look at how to manage the overall risks of investing

The purpose of diversification is to balance risks and opportunities and thus preserve and grow your capital. Certain types of financial assets thrive under conditions that cause other types to wither away. By thinking clearly about the conditions that cause some to wither and others to thrive, we can prepare our portfolios for potentially adverse conditions and stop worrying about the "what-ifs" of the global economy and geopolitical events.

My basic premise in the area of asset allocation is this: If you are primarily invested in *financial* assets (anything other than direct investment in real estate or other physical objects), the biggest threats and opportunities to your net worth are monetary. They are currency-related. (Or, at least historically speaking, the largest threats manifest themselves in currency-related trends.) This is because cash is the lifeblood of our system of economics, and because cash is no longer a physical asset like gold or silver it can be created out of thin air by the Federal Reserve Bank. It is therefore subject to the vagaries and political temptations of those who control the supply of money.

A review of history shows that while lately these mistakes have not been obvious in a major way, they do from time to time dominate the economic landscape, with tremendous implications. I believe the largest-portfolio-impacting events of the 20th century were (chronologically) (1) the deflation of the 1930s, (2) the inflation of the 1960s and 1970s, (3) the interest rate increases of the early 1980s, and (4) the disinflation and resulting decrease in interest rates of 1982-1998. All of these had tremendous impact, both good and bad, on the portfolios of investors in the United States, and all were currency-related events. Obviously, it makes sense to at least be ready for the recurrence of these or similar events in the future.

Using history as our guide, it would seem that the biggest threats and opportunities for our portfolios are either (1) excessive inflation, (2) deflation—any amount of which is excessive, or (3) growth without significant inflation or deflation. Normally, especially in recent years, conditions have favored scenario number three, the growth scenario, but the other two cannot be ruled out simply because they haven't happened lately. Keep in mind that when I say that currency-related issues are the biggest threats and opportunities, I am talking about *major* financial shifts, that is, once- or twice-in-a-lifetime occurrences.

Although proper asset allocation will certainly reduce the volatility of your portfolio during small shifts as well as large, it is in readiness for the possibility of major shifts that we hold different asset classes. Shifts from inflation to deflation or from deflation to growth are what can literally make you or break you. They don't happen very often, maybe once every 20 or 30 years, but, unfortunately, hardly anyone can ever see them coming. Do you plan on being alive 20 years from now? If so, you'd better be ready for any scenario.

Inflationary scenarios are normally unkind to stocks, because they cause uncertainty about whether companies will be able to grow earnings faster than the rate of inflation. Inflationary periods often create bear markets because companies are consumed with the necessity to pass price increases on to their customers. This concern with what is essentially a non-productive activity hinders innovation and growth. Inflation also tends to be associated with increasing interest rates as the central bank tries to bring inflation under control—and higher rates are rarely good for stocks.

Investors have come to expect that some degree of price inflation is built into our system, but whenever inflation starts to creep above 4 percent, both investors and the Federal Reserve Bank tend to get nervous. Much of this is because the inflationary problems in the 1970s and 80s are not so long ago, and we remember how the central bankers then let inflation run out of control for many years. Some nervousness arises because it is well understood that our currency has no inherent value; its value depends on the abilities of those who control the supply of dollars, the members of the Federal Reserve Board. And of course, investors in stock realize the indisputable relationship between inflation, interest rates, and the stock market.

Deflation is not good for stocks, either, because a shrinking economy almost always causes reduced sales, and therefore reduced profits. It does bring lower interest rates, but only when those lower rates result in increased economic activity is there any hope for the earnings of companies to rise. Notable examples of deflationary circumstances were the Great Depression of the 1930s and the problems in Japan starting in the 1990s.

The scenario we as investors hope for is growth without significant inflation or deflation. As long as price levels for consumer goods are stable, there is no reason for the Fed to tinker with interest rates (although it usually does anyway).

Why all this discussion of inflation and deflation, and the Goldilocks scenario of "just right" growth with stable currency value? Simply because, if we want our portfolios to be bulletproof and yet provide a good return, we have to build them in a way that addresses all three potential scenarios. How do we do that? First, let's list exactly which types of investments do well and which do poorly in each currency environment:

Excessive Inflation. Big-time losers in periods of high inflation will be bonds, especially long-term bonds, because the principal and interest will be paid back to you in inflated, and therefore less valuable, dollars than those you paid for the securities. The shares of most companies, both industrial and service, will also lose out due to concerns about their ability to pass ever-increasing costs through to consumers. Investments that do well are producers of commodities and holders of real assets, such as Real Estate Investment Trusts (REITs) and integrated oil companies. In inflationary times, their goods are readily salable at ever-rising prices, while the majority of their costs are fixed.

Deflation. In deflationary times, hardly anything does well except high-quality, long-term, non-callable bonds. Long-term U.S. Treasury bonds with 10- to 30-year maturities are the assets of choice then, especially in a tax-deferred account such as an IRA. Depending on your tax situation, you may want to consider longer-term, insured general obligation municipal bonds, which receive favorable tax treatment and have low credit risk. Deflation causes interest rates to drop (which raises the prices and therefore the market value of bonds), with the added benefit that principal and interest will be paid back to the bondholder in dollars that have increased purchasing power.

Be careful, though. Many corporate and municipal bonds are callable. That is, they can be refinanced at the whim of the issuer, and these do not tend to increase in value as much as non-callable bonds when interest rates are dropping. Moreover, corporate bonds do not enjoy the safety rating of Treasuries, a factor of considerable importance in poor economic times. Even mortgage-backed bonds (GNMA—"Ginnie Maes" as they are called), which are called back as people refinance their mortgages at lower rates, do not do much for an investor in periods of deflation.

Be especially careful to avoid junk bonds in deflationary times. A tough economy calls into serious question the ability of debt-laden firms to repay what they owe to bondholders.

Stocks of all types do poorly in true deflationary times, as deflation and recession are always found together, depressing corporate earnings.

Growth Without Significant Inflation or Deflation. When the central bankers get monetary policy right, the result is that wonderful scenario where inflation stays positive but very low, and the economy and corporate earnings grow steadily. In this environment, bonds may be stable or decrease slightly in price, while commodities will have no discernible trend in any direction. Stock prices give a very good return in this situation.

A WELL-PREPARED ASSET ALLOCATION

Taking all this into account, I propose the approximate allocation of assets to minimize risk and maximize return that is shown in Table 2-1.

TABLE 2-1. ASSET ALLOCATION EXAMPLE

Asset Type	Approximate Allocation/ Percent of Portfolio	Function
Growth stocks,* broadly diversified among many industries. Mix of large- and small-capitalization companies. Some portion of these all to be actively managed.	55 percent	Earnings and share prices grow with the economy. For the "growth without inflation" scenario.
Long-Term Treasury bonds (or possibly longer-term, insured municipal bonds with minimal call features). Emphasis is on high credit quality.	35 percent	Increase in price during deflationary periods, offsetting losses in other categories. Give a reasonable return in most economic circumstances.
Gold stocks	6 percent	These defensive issues are our portfolio's inflation hedge. They give a decent return in normal times, but do best during inflationary periods.
Integrated oil producers (or natural resource stocks).	2 percent	
Real Estate Investment Trusts (REITS)	2 percent	
Total	100 percent	

* *Diversify between many disparate industry groups, or buy a mutual fund that does the same.*

Obviously, this is a cursory look at asset allocation, intended merely to get you thinking about the actual scenarios your portfolio may face, rather than just the ones that the financial press may be talking about at the moment. Asset allocation is a complicated subject; many factors need to be considered before you can arrive at an allocation suitable to your unique needs. Among these are your age, your tolerance for risk, how much money you have, when you will need to use the money, and your current income from other sources.

What is important is that you be prepared for all three major monetary scenarios. Too many people tend to ignore the inflationary or deflationary scenarios until they are already upon them, which is too late. The successful investor prepares for scenarios other than just the ones that have occurred in the past 20 years.

With an allocation of resources that protects you from monetary risks, your portfolio should be able to weather any of the major economic circumstances that can reasonably be anticipated, continuing to give you a good return during the majority of times. Although a well-constructed portfolio may not balance out the entire decline in a bear market, for instance, it will balance out much of it. All these investments are leveraged in the sense that they can really take off in the right environment. For instance, gold stocks have certainly not been associated with tremendous returns lately (due to low inflation in recent years and the fact that the central bank has been selling gold), but a hypothetical 10 percent increase in the price of gold would cause a 30 percent to 50 percent increase in the value of gold-mining stocks. The same is true of oil, and, to some extent real estate trust holdings. And in a deflationary environment, long-term Treasury bond values can increase substantially in value to offset losses on other classes of assets.

When choosing bonds or bond mutual funds, for our purposes here, find the longer maturities and the highest credit quality available to get maximum leverage should interest rates fall in a protracted deflation. Since the bond portion of our hypothetical portfolio is only 35 percent, you want the maximum change in value for any given change in interest rates. Again, I repeat: Avoid junk and callable bonds. Concentrate on non-callable, long-term Treasury securities. Our purpose is for bonds to act as a buffer against deflation during difficult economic conditions—something that only the highest-credit-quality, longest-term issues can accomplish.

All the classes of assets I've mentioned are available through mutual funds. Almost every fund family has broadly diversified stock funds, U.S. Treasury or municipal bond funds, REIT sector funds, oil and energy funds, and gold stock funds. But buying individual securities is always an alternative.

Consider rebalancing your portfolio back to the recommended percentages every few years, though not too often. Cycles of inflation, deflation, and economic growth take years to play out, and you want the portion of your portfolio that is doing well under each condition to have time to compound its gains.

I recognize that the reason you are reading this book is to learn how to make money using a portfolio of individual stocks. That being the case, your actively managed portfolio of individual stocks will be some portion of the 55 percent or so that you have invested in growth stocks. The balance of this book is devoted to explaining how to select and manage individual high-profit-potential stocks.

CHAPTER SUMMARY

Don't lose sight of the importance of good asset allocation. Keep a long and broad view of monetary conditions that periodically crop up during most lifetimes. History does repeat itself; as investors we need to be students of history and prepare accordingly: Be prepared for inflation, deflation, and growth conditions at all times, no matter how unlikely each may seem to be. This preparation will give you the confidence to hold onto the winning investments in the aggressive portion of your portfolio during the inevitable sharp, temporary corrections.

CHAPTER 3 ━━━━━━━━
THREE CRITICAL SURVIVAL SKILLS

This chapter covers a top-level overview of the three most critical skills for the professional, active investor: diversification, risk control, and highly targeted stock picking. There are lots of rules and skills an investor can learn, but most of them fall under, or are subordinate to, these three major skill sets.

DIVERSIFICATION

Have you ever read the heart-breaking news stories that appear from time to time about some retired couple that lost their life savings when they entrusted everything to a swindler? It is instructive to learn from the mistakes of others, but what lesson is to be learned from this? Some people decide they should never trust anyone with anything, but personally I reject this conclusion. For most of us to go through life not trusting anyone would not only be difficult or impossible, it would be a downright miserable way to live.

What, then, should we learn from the mistakes of these unfortunate people? These sad stories are excellent illustrations of rule number one of investing—diversify. In fact, the main mistake made by people who lose everything is almost always a failure to diversify. This is true whether the person is a multimillionaire or a person of average means. There are exceptions, of course, and I don't mean to suggest that we shouldn't be compassionate toward those who have fallen on hard times. Hard times can happen to anyone; our goal should be to decrease the odds of it happening to us to as low a level as possible. If you put all your eggs in one basket, you're increasing, not decreasing, the odds. This is why Chapter 2 on asset allocation is included in a book primarily devoted to successful stock investment.

The subconscious mind can help in many ways to alert us to dangers. If at any time you ever feel you have so much riding on one particular security or outcome that you cannot be comfortable, better look again at how well you've diversified. It's probably not enough. As Jesse Livermore advised, "Sell down to the sleeping point."[1] You must at all times let reason rule over greed or fear, but especially greed, which can cause you to take too much risk. In the stock market, you usually find yourself tempted to be greediest just when the risk is greatest.

RISK CONTROL AND LOSS-CUTTING: A CRITICAL KEY TO SURVIVAL

Investing in stocks is like finding a seat in a crowded theatre: You always want to be near the exit in case something unforeseen happens. The only difference is that the likelihood of something bad happening to one of your stocks is far higher than the likelihood that you'll ever be caught in a burning theatre.

Next to diversification, the most essential skill that any aggressive investor can acquire is the ability to live with a loss, or, put another way, to control losses. Even the world's worst stock-picker may eventually happen onto some very large winners. And even the best will inevitably happen onto some big losers. Find a way to minimize their effects and you can save yourself the misery of devastating losses while still scoring some incredible gains. The goal of loss-cutting is not to save you from all losses but to save you from the tragic, unrecoverable loss.

THE LOSS CONTROL PLAN

The almost always-neglected aspect of investing is the third skill, planning for loss control. This is the document that is the overarching guide for your investment actions. Everything else that you do has to be guided by this document. The loss-control plan gives the professional investor

---

[1]Edwin Lefevre, *Reminiscences of a Stock Operator.* New York: John Wiley & Sons, Inc., 1994.

something tangible with which to control not just risk but also loss-generating behaviors. This plan is discussed in detail in Chapter 4.

LOSS-CUTTING

During the bullish 1990s, many people forgot the need to cut losses. They fell into the fallacy that profits would continue uninterrupted, forever. "Buy and hold" advocates were hailed as geniuses, as they always are at the crest of a bull market.

Now that the new millennium bear market has put that idea to rest (for a while, at least), many investors are afraid to commit whatever capital they have left to growth companies.

Investors who have not used the bear market as an opportunity to learn better money management techniques *should* fear to reenter the market; they would do well to stay away. Fear can be a good thing, saving us from making foolish moves when there is danger. In large part, fear of investing is entirely rational after an experience of losing a great deal of money, especially for those who have no means of controlling risk. More profoundly, the fear is especially rational for those who don't even have a clue about what they did to deserve such a fate in the first place.

Sadly, the vast majority of investors simply have no exit plan for a stock when they buy it. Either they're naturally optimistic, or they simply cannot bear to prepare for the possibility that their stock will decline. Playing into this is the fact that they don't know how to protect themselves. Hence, over time they naturally lose some money when bad times hit a particular company they are holding, and they lose huge amounts when bad times hit all companies. The juvenile who says, "He who fights and runs away, lives to fight another day" is easily adapted to real life in the stock market. Unfortunately, few investors heed this simple wisdom.

Every serious investor knows the necessity of limiting losses; indeed, over the years much has been written on the subject. My first real exposure to loss-cutting ideas was in Edwin Lefevre's book, *Reminiscences of a Stock Operator* and Gerald M. Loeb's series of books from the 1960s and 1970s.[2] Many authors have set percentage loss parameters of between 5 percent and 10 percent, meaning that if one of your stocks declines from your purchase point by that much, you should sell and move on to another stock.

---

[2] Gerald M. Loeg, *Your Battle for Stock Market Profits.* New York: Simon & Schuster, 1971.

I want to challenge you to think of loss-cutting in a different way: In common sense terms, the critical thing is not what percentage loss you may take on any one stock but the percentage of your *portfolio value* that is risked, whether on any one trade or in total. Assume you have $50,000 of equity in your brokerage account; you take a maximum position of $5,000 in a single stock (10 percent of your account value). Further, you determine to limit your loss on each position to 10 percent: if your first buy was 100 shares of XYZ Corp. at $50 a share ($5,000 total value without commissions), then you would place a stop-loss order at $45/share. If you were unfortunate enough to be stopped out on this stock at $45/share, you would lose about 1 percent of your total portfolio value ($500). A loss, sure, and probably psychologically painful—but a very manageable loss from the standpoint of the portfolio as a whole. If you had invested your entire $50,000 into a single stock (1,000 shares) and taken a loss at $45/share, the entire portfolio would now be down 10 percent ($5,000) , which I consider to be a serious percentage loss. That's why I highly advocate controlling risk by limiting investments in a single stock to a small percentage of the total portfolio value. I would never want to risk more than 3 percent of my portfolio value on any one trade, and I strive to limit it to 1 percent most of the time.

Extending this thinking on controlling losses, the loss-control plan described in Chapter 4 is the foundation of your investment ventures and an integral part of the system of investing you'll learn about here.

HOW LACK OF AN EXIT PLAN HURTS YOUR PERFORMANCE

Devastating losses are one thing that can destroy stock performance for most investors—and they are almost always a direct result of the investor's failure to decide before entering a trade how she will exit it. Since the potential gains from a stock are always higher than the potential losses (100 percent loss potential versus unlimited upside potential), an even bigger source of underperformance is selling too soon when you do find a great winner.

An exit plan is one thing that experienced investors/traders *always* have before initiating a position. The reason is simple: Unless you have a plan and stick to it, every decision you make will be emotional, not rational. Worse yet, the larger your position, the more emotional and less rational your decision making. It is vital to make all your exit decisions up front, at the moment of acquisition, before you get scared (if the stock starts to head down) or greedy (if it soars). Emotional decisions almost always are poor ones, leading to large losses and small gains. I never, ever enter a stock position without immediately setting up a corresponding sell-stop.

The pitfalls of trying to manage a stock portfolio without a plan are many and varied. Friends, stockbrokers, market advisors, and the like are all likely to give you advise that has a magnifying effect on the natural fear and greed that are present in every investor. These influences can cause someone who does not have a well-thought-out plan to abandon profitable positions and hang on to losing ones—exactly why the majority of amateur investment dabblers under perform the market: they do not have a plan of any kind. The old saying, "When you fail to plan, you plan to fail," is as true in the stock market as in any other aspect of life.

With emotions running rampant from prospects of either a loss or a large gain, it is virtually impossible to make a good decision. This is precisely the point at which most investors fail: Because they have no preconceived plan for exiting a stock before they buy it, whenever they hear a tip or rumor on a stock, they get so excited that they forget to ask themselves what they will do to cut their losses if it turns sour, or if it soars, how will they let the profit ride?

The chances of a good decision by an investor who doesn't plan ahead and also believes some of the myths of the market are almost nil. If you are a decision-maker of any kind, you no doubt realize that making decisions based on wrong assumptions make your chances of success minuscule. That's why the importance of an exit plan based on sound theory before a stock purchase cannot be overemphasized. Unfortunately, when they're buying a stock most investors don't want to think about planning ahead (especially for the possibility that it will head south), so they put off setting the selling criteria until it's unavoidable. Then, it's usually too late.

We live in a wonderful age where it's possible to place sell-stop orders on just about any equity security, even on over-the-counter issues. This was not true even 10 years ago, but it is now. So why not use this tremendous tool and resolve never to buy another stock without placing a sell order at the same time? Later in this book, you'll learn exactly where to place these orders for maximum effect. For now, simply assimilate *when* to place them, and that is *immediately* after you buy any stock.

In the next chapter, we will have a more detailed discussion of loss-cutting techniques and the most important concepts pertaining to risk control, which is by far the most critical discipline in investing.

HIGHLY TARGETED STOCK-PICKING

In the best of times (like most of the past 20 years) stock-picking skills were optional. The rising tide of market returns indeed lifted most, if not all, ships. But going forward, for his continued well-being the professional investor cannot afford to bank on a repeat of such glory times.

For professionally-minded investors willing to pay attention to actual market trends and willing to tune out the popular but misguided preoccupation with the top 100 tech stocks, there are always plenty of opportunities for profit. Even during the past year, while investors in the NASDAQ 100 watched their value plummet by 29 percent, the distribution of returns shown in Table 3-1 were available.

TABLE 3-1: STOCK RETURNS—6,115 STOCKS AT OVER $1.00 PER SHARE (APRIL 26, 2001 – APRIL 26, 2002)

One Year Stock Return	Number of Stocks	% of Total Universe
0% to 9.9%	588	9.6%
10% to 19.9%	564	9.2%
20% to 29.9%	492	8.0%
30% to 39.9%	369	6.0%
40% to 49.9%	339	5.5%
50% to 99.9%	706	11.5%
100% to 199.9%	339	5.5%
200% and up	130	2.1%
Total positive returns	3,527	57.7%

Source: Yahoo! Finance Stock Screener

Those who were too busy concerning themselves with the misery of their former darling tech stocks probably missed out altogether on the actual, fairly positive returns enjoyed in less well-known stocks. This most recent period points up the rewards of highly selective stock-picking, and how focusing on major market indexes can blind you to what's actually happening.

To profit in the current environment, you must sniff out the *actual* performers, not somehow hope that the stocks you are familiar with will come back. The old performers probably won't be performers again for a long, long time. The stocks that are heavily represented in the market averages (e.g., the large technology stocks) have fallen into a period of underperformance, and any serious student of market history knows that trying to guess when underperformance will end rarely succeeds. Industry sectors historically have fallen into and out of favor in very long cycles of 10 to 20 years. At this point, few investors remember the long period in the 1970s and 1980s when tech stocks under performed, and even fewer believe it could happen again. Yet, it *may* happen again. Certainly, there will be technology stocks that perform very well over the coming decade. All bear markets come to an end. But when they do, it may be the currently unheard-of tech stocks that come back the best, not the well-known ones.

This book will show you a process for letting the market itself tell you which stocks to invest in, rather than relying on the headlines or, even worse, relying on investing only in companies you've heard of.

Just as the percentage of your portfolio that you risk on a single trade is important, your win/loss ratio is also important. In fact, these two things together do more to determine your overall results than anything else. All stocks are *not* created equal. You must remember this if you want to profit handsomely in stocks. Generally, we want to buy stocks that have a high potential for growth. If you think about it, this will in most cases exclude large, established companies in mature industries. It may, however, include companies with smaller market share in mature industries, if they are changing the paradigm in their industry through innovative approaches in manufacturing, marketing, or services. It may also mean larger companies in the more dynamic industries.

Small-company and large-company stocks have long periods where one group outperforms the other; try to keep aware of which phase you are in at any given point. But essentially, if you want the potential for high rewards, you must be willing to put your money either with lesser-known companies that are not already dominant in their industries, or with emerging industries. "No risk, no reward," as the saying goes, and it is especially true in the stock market. In order to make money, there must be ways of *managing* the risks of such investments, and that is what this book is all about.

Over recent decades, most stocks participated in the tremendous rallies of U.S. equity securities. Going forward, this may not be true; at least, the returns from the general market may be lower, resulting in the need to be more selective in choosing stocks that may have the possibility of giving an extraordinarily good return. No matter what happens with the indexes, there will still be many, many tremendous gainers. In this book, how to find them is addressed in a way that is not highly subjective, as it is in many other books on the subject. Chapter 8 presents all you will need to know to get your stock picks in sync with the market, and in so doing, stack the odds greatly in your favor.

CHAPTER SUMMARY

The serious or professional investor recognizes that surviving and prospering means always having a portfolio that is properly diversified, having a loss control plan and cutting losses on every position, and understanding what criteria are most important for picking high-potential stocks. These are the essential skills of the person who is not willing to entrust her financial future to passive investing. As you read this book, you will learn not just how to build every one of these skills, but also how to apply them.

CHAPTER 4 ――――――
CAPITAL PRESERVATION CONCEPTS

Nearly every book on stock investing written in the past 50 years recommends a specific percentage loss allowance for each stock. Some recommend setting your stop-order no more than 5 percent, 8 percent, or 10 percent below your purchase price. While the admonition to cut losses quickly is laudable, the advice is highly incomplete.

I encourage you to think more about the maximum risk to your portfolio, not just about a set percentage for each position. In other words, start to think in terms of what percentage of your total *account value* is at risk at any time. This may seem like a subtle difference, but it isn't. For example, people whose only capital preservation concept is limiting losses to 10 percent of any trade may be misled into taking positions that are too large. If they devoted 100 percent of their account value to one stock, set their loss-limitation to 10 percent, and had three consecutive failed trades, their entire account would be down close to 27 percent—a very large loss on an overall account basis. And it is *very* easy to be stopped out of a position when placing stops only 5 percent or 10 percent away from the purchase price.

IN LOSS CONTROL, ACCOUNT DRAWDOWN IS THE CRUCIAL CONCEPT

When the value of your account falls from its peak by a certain percentage, this drop in value is known as *drawdown*. Where loss control is concerned, this is the most important concept. The fact that you limited your losses on each trade to 10 percent of that trade's value will be little comfort if your account value has dropped 30 percent from a series of unsuccessful trades.

At all times, understand what your maximum risk is if all your positions are stopped out. Have a maximum dollar amount that you are willing to risk on any trade, no matter how wonderful the company you are buying into may seem. Use your account value to derive this dollar amount. For instance, on an account worth $100,000, you may want to limit yourself to a maximum 3 percent loss on any one trade. This would translate into a $3,000 maximum loss you are willing to take on any company you buy into. Suppose you decide arbitrarily to set your sell-stop-orders at 15 percent below your purchase price on every trade; you would then determine your position size, as follows:

$3,000 maximum per-position risk divided by 0.15 equals: $20,000 maximum position size per trade.

You should also define how much loss in account drawdown you are willing to take. This is the total of all risk to the position—in other words, the purchase price minus the stop price times the total number of shares.

Using the same example, where an investor has a maximum loss tolerance of $3,000 per position: If the maximum account drawdown tolerance for this investor were 10 percent, that would imply no more than three positions of $20,000 each, for a total of $60,000 invested in three stocks. Obviously, an account with 60 percent of its assets devoted to three stocks would be a highly concentrated portfolio, but we are using this merely as an example, not as a model. If the investor were stopped out of all three positions at a loss of $3,000 each, the total loss would be $9,000, within the investor's 10 percent ($10,000) maximum drawdown tolerance.

In reality, rather than devote a $100,000 account to just three positions with a maximum combined risk of $9,000, the rational investor would want to have, say, 10 to 20 positions totaling $60,000. This would give a much better level of diversification than just three stocks and a much better chance of hitting at least one great winner. Remember, the maximum drawdown tolerance is just that—a maximum. You do not have to position your portfolio to expose it to the maximum risk you are willing to tolerate, especially when you are just starting out. To do so will put too much pressure on you, and this type of pressure seldom brings out the best in a person. It will attack your judgment and discipline (defined as being able to adhere to your investment system at all times).

MAXIMUM POSITION LOSS AND MAXIMUM DRAWDOWN TOLERANCE

THE LOSS CONTROL PLAN

Before buying even one stock, each investor has to decide on a maximum loss tolerance. Are you willing to risk 10 percent, 20 percent, even more, of your account? Decide and write it down. If you don't write it down, you'll forget it in a moment of bullish euphoria, and before you know it, you'll be in over your head. Loss tolerance is the basic building block for the rest of your portfolio.

Walking through an example, let's look at an investor who has just put $50,000 in an account for buying individual equities. She dutifully writes down her plan for limiting her risk, as follows:

Loss Control Plan

1. Account principal: $50,000

2. Maximum drawdown tolerance (percent): 15 percent

3. Maximum drawdown tolerance (line 1 x line 2): $7,500

4. Anticipated stop-loss percentage (chosen arbitrarily as an example): 20 percent

5. Maximum account value to be risked on any one trade: 2 percent

6. Maximum dollar value to be risked on any one trade (line 1 x line 5): $1,000

7. Expected number of positions (line 3/line 6): 7.5

8. Targeted size of positions (line 6/line 4): $5,000

The investor now has a plan for controlling loss in her entire portfolio. She can add seven positions of $5,000 each, and place a 20 percent stop-loss for each position. This does not guarantee that she won't lose the 15 percent maximum drawdown tolerance, but it does greatly reduce the chances of losing more than this. Even if she foolishly decides to add all the positions at the same time, at a very bad time (the start of a bear market) and gets stopped out of every position, she will lose the $7,500 maximum loss tolerance. It's a safe bet, though, that if she didn't take the time to write down even this simple plan, she would have committed too much, and lost even more.

There are several morals to this story, but the major one is: *The time to think about how much you are willing to lose is before you take even one position.* The loss control plan is the starting point for doing this. Take the time to give it serious thought, write it down, calculate it, and honor it.

I'll discuss where to place sell-stop orders later, in Chapters 10 and 13.

CHAPTER SUMMARY

The loss control plan is the starting point for any well-founded investment plan. Always draw one up before you embark on buying individual stocks. It will help you to recognize and control the risks you're taking in your portfolio while you can still do something about it. Think long and hard about the maximum loss you would be willing to assume, and don't just assume that the worst case will not occur. Start to think in terms of the maximum impact a single trade could have on your total account, and try to limit it to just one to 3 percent of your account value.

Of equal importance. After you construct your loss control plan, you must have the discipline to adhere to it. A good plan ignored is as bad as no plan at all.

CHAPTER 5
TWO BASIC INVESTOR PROFILES

Investing, whether by individuals for their own account or by professionals, is largely a psychological discipline. True, different investors have different styles and always will have, but beyond mere style lies something more basic, something that profoundly affects our success or failure as investors. That something is the motive force, the reason *why* we invest in the first place.

Although we all believe we invest to make money, which is not always the case. From my observation, most investors seem to be motivated by two factors in varying degrees, ego and money. I'm convinced these two motives are the most instructive for us to study in order to learn to recognize our own follies.

Let's deal with two basic profiles: the ego-driven investor and the results-oriented investor. The ego-driven investor is self-destructive, the results-oriented investor is self-instructive. Like it or not, each of us has inborn traits characteristic of both types. The irony is that if you feel you have none of the traits of the ego-driven investor, by definition you probably have many of them. It is my hope that presenting these profiles will help you analyze yourself, identify destructive ego-driven traits, and correct them.

THE EGO-DRIVEN INVESTOR

The ego-driven investor sees investing as exciting. He makes investments as a way to garner the respect and admiration of others. He may also see investing as entertainment. He is constantly talking about this or that great deal, trying to impress others, or himself, with his prowess and immense wisdom. In reality, he probably doesn't really make much money in the stock market, a fact that he hides from the outside world by every means possible.

Worst of all, the ego-driven type never gets any better at investing. To admit he has been doing something wrong, even to himself, is more than his sensitive ego can take. Since the aura of being an investment wizard is simply a way for him to gain affirmation from others, he really doesn't care much about the results as long as he can stay in the game and keep talking about his smart deals at cocktail parties. Conveniently forgetting the bad deals, he keeps turning over in his mind his best deals and how smart he must be. He certainly never performs an autopsy on any of his losing trades to figure out just why they were losers. He may blame losses on his broker, the company's management, bad luck, or stock manipulators. He can't learn anything new, because to ask anyone else what he may have done wrong would be to admit he's made a mistake.

One way such an investor deals with losses is by stubbornly holding on to losing stocks, no matter how far they drop. He reasons that until he sells, he hasn't really lost anything, so why lose face by selling? Never mind that every month his account statements tell him how much his account value has dwindled—he really *has* lost money, whether or not he admits it or not. In this way he ensures that he can never redeploy what's left of his capital into something more promising.

The ego-driven investor doesn't enjoy buying a stock that has already doubled in value; even if it could go on to increase another 1,000 percent. The idea that someone else was "smarter" than him and bought at a lower price wounds his pride. On the other hand, he dearly loves to buy stocks that arc on a downtrend because there's a chance that he will be the one who will buy the stock at its low for the year. Imagine the bragging rights associated with such an accomplishment! Of course, most of the time when he buys these types of stocks, they just keep going down, down, down. But that's OK, because no one in his circle of friends knows about these deals. The prospect of that unlikely but alluring "buying the bottom" scenario keeps him coming back for more.

Even when he does get lucky and happens to stumble into a winner, the ego-driven investor is his own worst enemy. He waits until the stock hits a new high for the year and then promptly sells out to lock in his profit. Meanwhile, this stock was in an uptrend and keeps right on sailing, far above where he exited. Or he may hold onto a winner long after it has started to fade, because he wants that opportunity to "sell the top." Sometimes he holds on so long that his profit evaporates completely.

Thus, the ego-driven investor's system is complete: He always holds onto losing stocks and when something starts to go right, he bails out or holds on till the uptrend has ended and a downturn starts. He has plenty to talk about at parties, but there is no way he can ever make a decent profit. Since he blames others for all his problems, his results will never get any better.

THE RESULTS-ORIENTED INVESTOR

The results-oriented investor seldom talks with others about his investment results; he's too busy trying to make them better. He is never too proud to buy a stock that is making new highs, realizing that those who are buying the stock most likely know far more than he does—and a winning company is more likely to keep on winning than a losing company is to start winning. He does his homework on a company's prospects, but he doesn't argue with the market itself. The fact that someone else was smarter and bought at a lower price doesn't worry him; it's against his nature even for such a thought to occur to him. He's far too busy trying to pick stocks that are performing well. He strives to achieve his "personal best," and compares his performance against others' performance only as a way to learn and get better.

When the results-oriented investor finds himself with a stock that's zooming ahead, he holds on, letting the stock continue to do well for him. Conversely, when a stock stumbles badly enough that his loss-control plan says it's time to exit, he acts without hesitation. He follows his plan for buying and selling whether that means selling at a gain or at a loss. He also never sells a stock as it's making a new high; since his concern is not to sell the top but to let his winning positions run their course.

One huge difference between the results-oriented and the ego-driven investor is what the former does with losses. While the ego-driven investor blames others and learns nothing, the results-oriented person studies in great detail how the loss occurred, and eventually finds the fallacies in his thinking or his system. Thus, he always gets better and better at what he is doing. In fact, he even keeps a notebook on each loss and records what he could have done better.

CHAPTER SUMMARY

Know yourself. Understand your motives for being an investor and try to emulate the results-oriented investor, not the ego-driven one. Keep records and analyze them to understand where ingrained ideas or habits may be minimizing your results.

CHAPTER 6
THE INVESTOR'S MENTALITY: FALLACIES TO ELIMINATE

FALLACY #1: FINANCIAL ANALYSIS IS THE KEY TO PROFITABLE STOCK INVESTING

I first became interested in investing in 1979 while taking investment and securities analysis classes as I worked on my degree in finance. After this, I had a few years of frustration as I bought stocks that had good financial and industry characteristics (just as I'd been taught), but that didn't do any better than the average stock—and some did far worse. There didn't seem to be any predictive value to my analyses, or anyone else's, for that matter.

In the early 1980s I was fortunate enough to happen onto several books written by persons who had actually made money in the stock market and was impressed with the fact that many of the most successful investors had no training whatsoever in finance or business. Not only that, they never even seemed to take financial ratios and such into account when they were looking for things to invest in. One, which particularly impressed me, was an old book by a professional dancer named Nicholas Darvas, who was well-documented as having turned about $10,000 into $2 million within a few years.[1]

This mystified me. Here was a man who knew nothing about finance or business, yet was astoundingly successful. If understanding finance was the key to profiting in stocks (as I believed at that point), how could

---

[1] Nicholas Darvas, *How I Made $2,000,000 in the Stock Market*. New York: Kensington Publishing Corp., 1986.

he have done it? To top things off, he was a constant world traveler and could only monitor the market via telegrams from his broker. All he could do, all he knew to do, was to monitor the trend of stocks and look for volume breakouts from consolidations and new trading highs as signals about which stocks to buy.

At some point, I concluded that his approach was more practical than the financial ratio and industry analysis that I had learned in business school. My results improved greatly, and very quickly.

Although it seems obvious to me now, just as you can't drive your car forward by looking through the rearview mirror, you can't predict future stock prices by analyzing past financial data alone. The stock market is heavily psychologically driven. That may not be provable with hard data, but it's a safe bet that most of the time, "value" and price are only very loosely connected. Sales and profits do determine the direction of the price trend in a company's stock, but psychology determines how far the trend goes.

Darvas, looking primarily at the price trend and volume of certain stocks, made a fortune. He knew that while all information is historical, whether it's accounting data or trading history, the trend of a stock's price is the market's aggregate consensus on the company's *future*. The accounting profession, appropriately, makes no attempt to assess the future prospects of a company; it only generates data about the past.

For the investor, this is of vital importance. Why? Because the fallacy that studying balance sheets and income statements is the key to profits in the stock market is at the heart of a common mistake. It's why investors gravitate toward low price/earning (P/E) stocks, stocks with "great financials," which are often stocks that are drifting or declining in price. Because these types of stocks, in fact, have diminishing growth prospects and should have little psychological appeal, clinging to this fallacy dooms a person to substandard investment performance.

FALLACY #2: BUY STOCKS IN GOOD COMPANIES AND HOLD THEM

"Good companies" can be a bad investment. Fantastically positive and consistent returns from stocks during the past two decades fostered the belief that some companies are so solid and so unassailable that they're a sure bet. The foundational assumption of this mistaken idea is that the market is so efficient that it will never let you buy a company for a price too far above its true value, so all you need to do is to find companies that have an outstanding market position and outstanding management, buy them, and sit back and grow rich.

How many times have we heard the seemingly wise investment advice: "Buy good companies and hold them"? The tragedy of this advice is that the amateur investor (and often professionals, too) almost always implements this maxim as "Buy the *best-known* companies and hold them." This 1990s herd mentality is mirrored in the 1960s, when the Nifty Fifty (the "good companies" of that time) were referred to as "one-decision growth stocks"—a person supposedly had only to make one decision, buy, and would never need to sell, never need to consider cutting losses. Most of these stocks under performed for decades after this.

The other tragedy of this popular idea is the assumption that some companies are so good that you don't need an exit plan to work with in case the share price starts to run into trouble. For the professional investor, there is no such thing as a company that good. Many of these companies undoubtedly have outstanding prospects as *businesses,* but doesn't mean they have outstanding prospects as *investments*. It's very difficult for mega capitalization companies to grow faster than the general economy, especially when as a group they are the largest, and slowest growing, slice of the general economy.

By definition, speculation in individual stocks is fraught with more variability and risk (and potentially more reward, of course) than investing in mutual funds. But history clearly shows that the failure to cut losses, even on "good" companies, eventually leaves investors in individual securities stuck holding lackluster performers, waiting for them to come back. No company is so well established that its stocks are unassailable. The most established companies sometimes go away entirely—to the surprise of everyone. More common, though, is the scenario where Wall Street falls in love (an emotional, not a rational choice) with a company, driving its price to absurd levels. It's always wise to allow for the worst case: Keep an exit plan for *every* stock in your portfolio, even "good" ones. And follow it.

No matter how well or poorly founded, every stock selection system produces both losers and winners. Losers should be discarded without regard to how wonderful the company is, and this book will tell you when to do this in no uncertain terms.

The time when you can think most clearly about why you would sell a stock is *before* it's bought. Until you own it, you have no emotional attachment to it, which means you can make totally rational decisions. Once you own something, as I've said, the temptation is to get either greedy or scared. These emotions can lead to a desire to lock in profits, so that you prematurely cut off an ascending price trend. More seriously, they also lead to a failure to do the right thing—cut the loss—when it's clear that the stock has entered a bearish phase.

The lesson? Do not buy into the idea of buying good companies and holding them. You need to cut losses when the system you're using shows that an individual stock investment has entered into a downtrend, no matter how "good" the company is presumed to be. For the investor, there are no good companies, only good stocks. No falling stock is a good one.

FALLACY #3: WHAT GOES DOWN MUST COME UP

If you want to find future Olympians, don't look in the intensive care unit. We all intuitively understand the absurdity of a coach shopping for competitive athletes in the intensive care unit. As an investor, you're the head coach, scouring the market for able performers for your portfolio. As in sports, you're likely find your most talented performers already in the big leagues, or at least rising stars in the minor leagues, with some people (not too many) already aware of their possibilities.

But somehow, when we enter the stock market, the common-sense approach we would use to find sports performers goes out the window. Some investors absolutely kill themselves, financially speaking, by scouring the new-lows list in the paper. Is that your tendency? Do you think you have to find performers that no one else yet recognizes, and that looking on the loser's list is the way to do it? I hope not.

To profit as an investor you have to find those companies that are *improving*. In other words, you need to find them after they begin advancing but before the CEO's face is on the cover of *Business Week* or *Forbes*. Avoid the new-lows list. Avoid stocks that even show a moderate downtrend. The talent scouts have seen these companies and concluded that they're not going to lead the pack. How likely is it that a minor-league under performer will become an overnight sensation? Think about that when you're tempted by an under performing company.

"Buy low, sell high"—that's the mantra every neophyte investor hears; it's probably the most common catch phrase about stock investment in our culture. What people need to understand is that buying low and selling high doesn't mean buying a declining stock. For the rational investor, there is only one essential outcome for any stock transaction: That the ultimate selling price is higher than the purchase price. It should not, and does not, matter whether the stock was bought after a decline in price or as it made a new record high.

I don't know who coined "Buy low, sell high," but generations of investors would have been better served if the phrase had been "Sell higher than you bought," or even, "Buy high and sell even higher." Human nature being what it is, though, it probably wouldn't have made much difference. There seems to be an innate tendency to want to buy a stock right at the bottom, ride it up, and sell at the top, even though that's nearly impossible. Maybe that's the appeal of it. In any case, this desire is not rational. It has probably lost more money for investors over the decades than any other inclination. If people were computers, they would only care about selling at a higher price than the purchase price. Although I wouldn't recommend being computer-like in other areas of life, in the area of investing it's probably not a bad idea!

Buying stocks that are in a downward price spiral is probably the most common mistake investors make, and it stems from this mistaken notion that what goes down is likely to come back up *within a reasonable amount of time.* In order to profit from such a system, you need to be right about two things at once (1) that the stock's slide will end (a surprisingly large number never do; they become worthless), and (2) when (and at what price) the stock's slide will end. Your chances of being right about both things are slim indeed. Being right about even one would be surprising.

The typical scenario for this particular mistake finds an investor scouring the stock pages for stocks near their 52-week lows, information that's readily available. They wrongly assume that if a stock is near its low for the year, it must be low for its worth, making this an opportune time to buy it. Bottom-fishers tend to find out too late just how easy it is for a stock to keep on making new 52-week lows.

As an aside, it's fairly common that a stock making a new 52-week high has as its 52-week low a price that was a 52-week *high* a year ago. That might seem like a confusing statement but if you think about it, it will make a lot of sense. If the stock has been in an uptrend for a year or more, the price that was once a new high will now be the lowest price for the past 52 weeks. Beginning investors usually don't even consider the possibility that this could be true, so they keep on buying dogs until their portfolio looks (and smells) like a kennel.

Often, investors convince themselves that buying a stock from the 52-week lows list is not a risky proposition because the price is low relative to past earnings, book value, or some other measure of "value." In reality, buying a downtrending stock is always risky, because you're betting against the entire market and its assessment of the company's earnings trend. Stocks make serious declines because market participants know something about the company's future earnings potential—something that you may not be aware of no matter how well you research the company. Seldom is the entire market wrong about these matters.

Sometimes the market *is* wrong, of course, but your chances of finding the exceptions are mighty slim because you're just one of thousands of people looking for them. It's very hard for one person to correctly second-guess the sum wisdom of thousands of other investors. Try to keep in mind that your objective is to maximize profits, not to outsmart the market. The two objectives are vastly different.

Another destructive outgrowth of the idea that what goes down must come up is adding more money to a losing position. The reasoning for this goes something like this: "I bought the stock when it was $40. Now it's $20, so it's twice as good a deal as it was at $40. Besides, my average cost per share will come way down once I add to the position." Sometimes this is called *dollar cost averaging (DCA)*—putting a certain dollar amount into a stock at specified time intervals or at specified price intervals when the stock drops in value.

When an investor adds to a position at equal time periods (e.g., $1,000 every quarter) independent of the price of the stock, I call it *time-based* dollar cost averaging. When an investor invests an equal dollar amount each time a stock declines in price by a certain level (e.g., $1,000 for each 20 percent decline in price), it's *price-based* dollar cost averaging (this practice, sometimes called *scale trading,* is discussed in Chapter 10). Time-based DCA makes a lot of sense if you diversify as you do it (for example, adding $200 per month to a diversified mutual fund), but price-based DCA makes no sense in any circumstance and is sure to bankrupt you if you do it consistently, especially with individual stocks. This is the most destructive of all investor mistakes.

The fallacy of price-based DCA can best be illustrated by an example. Diaz, who has decided to pursue price-based dollar cost averaging, picks a portfolio of 10 stocks and puts $10,000 into each stock, for a total investment of $100,000. Just for fun, let's assume we know ahead of time that one, but only one, of the stocks in Diaz's portfolio will decline until it becomes worthless (goes bankrupt) some time within the next year. Because Diaz is a devout price-based DCA advocate, his trading rule is that whenever the price of one of his stocks declines 50 percent, he will sell $5,000 worth of one of his better-performing stocks and use the proceeds to buy more shares in the declining stock. If the issue declines 50 percent from his second purchase point, he will sell another $5,000-worth of one of his other stocks and again add to this declining stock.

Can you guess what will happen to Diaz over the next year? It would be agonizing to watch, because, as you've probably guessed, Diaz's system will, over the course of the year, *automatically allocate all of his capital to the stock that is going bankrupt.* He will lose his entire $100,000 unless he has the good sense at some point to realize what a bloody poor system he has.

If you pursue a price-based DCA system consistently, eventually you will reach your Waterloo, as Diaz is about to. Eventually, everyone buys stocks in some company that's destined for the scrap heap, but when you do, cut the loss. Don't even think about adding to the position!

The practice of buying downtrending stocks is such a pervasive and tragic error that the importance of eliminating it from your bag of tricks cannot be overemphasized.

FALLACY #4: WHAT GOES UP MUST COME DOWN

The egotistical side of investors greatly fears being the "greatest fool"— the one who buys a stock just as it's topping out. That's why many people never profit from the really promising stocks that everyone eventually buys (assuming they're using the correct criteria for picking stocks). This ego-driven fear and lack of understanding of the persistence of stock trends (both downward and upward) leads to an unwillingness to pick stocks that may be near their high for the year. This mistake is not as serious as buying downtrending stocks, because buying downtrending stocks will lead to losses in your principal, while not buying strongly uptrending stocks will merely minimize your profits. However, since the objective of investing is to make money, either outcome is to be avoided!

Because "what goes up must come down" is certainly true in the natural world, it's often assumed to be true in the world of investing as well. Let me try to convince you that this assumption will lead you into significant strategic errors in your investing.

In the aggregate, stocks trend upward over time; at some point, they advance to the point where they will never again return to their previous levels. That is, they give investors a substantial and permanent return, just as investors in other types of assets demand and receive a permanent return. A good high-profile example of this is the Dow Jones Industrial Average, which is now at about 10,000. In the 1930s, it was around 50. I don't ever expect to see it at 50 again, although theoretically it's possible. From here the Dow may dive to 5,000, but there's a certain point below which it will never again dip, until the world, as we know it, comes to an end. So certainly the gains enjoyed by shareholders up to a certain level on the Dow may be considered "permanent." At some time in the future, too, the market will at some point dip to the 5,000 level for the last time, so these gains will become permanent. Naturally, there's no way to tell when that will happen. The psychological difficulty many people have is that there's no way to tell how much of the Dow's current level is permanent and how much is temporary.

Certainly, some individual stocks do go up rapidly, then give back the entire gain just as rapidly. All seasoned investors have had this type of disappointment. However disappointing it may be to see a good profit evaporate, don't let this bitter experience lead you to believe in taking profits too quickly. If you do, over time it will cost you the really big gains.

If you think about it, if the entire stock market marches higher, often never to return, there must of necessity be some individual stocks that also advance without returning to their previous lower price levels. In fact, this is the case more often than not. Even so, investors regularly express the belief that when they have a profit going they should take the money and run. They assume that the stock *must* at some point drop to its former levels. But that's not true at all.

The grain of truth in this myth is the fact that any stock trend consists of a series of advances and retreats, resulting in a net increase over time.

If you want to believe that "what goes up must come down," keep in mind that that a stock often moves *way, way* up, and then comes down just a little. If a stock increases tenfold in value and then there's a 20 percent correction, we are still ahead by eightfold.

Given enough time, stocks of individual companies often make substantial price progress, sometimes with no major pullbacks in price. In fact, Table 6-1 is a listing of just a few stocks whose prices increased remarkably over a period of years. (I have intentionally avoided 1995-2000, since these years were not typical).

TABLE 6-1: SOME STOCK MAKING MAJOR PRICE MOVES

Stock	Split-Adjusted Price Move	Time Period	Percentage Gain
Fastenal	$0.88 to $38.00	1987-95	4,242%
Linear Technology	$2.12 to $38.00	1989-95	1,688%
Jupiter National	$3.50 to $27.00	1991-93	671%
Mid-Atlantic Medical Services	$2.38 to $27.00	1991-94	1,078%
Micron Technology	$3.00 to $95.00	1992-95	3,066%

There are many, many others, in every decade. Obviously, these are the types of stocks you want to find and hold onto. You won't find all of them, but eventually you'll find some of them if you use the stock selection criteria in this book.

Let me also point out that all the stocks listed spent a lot of time on the daily new-highs list in your favorite financial newspapers, while they were increasing in value. Linear Technology, for example, hit a new 52-week high on January 3, 1990, at $2 3/4 (adjusted for subsequent stock splits). It stood at $45 5/8 on November 9, 1995. There were 1,491 trading days between those two dates, during which Linear Technology appeared on the new-highs list 157 times—an average of about once every two weeks. During those 1,491 trading days, Linear Technology did not appear on the 52-week lows list even once. Yet, incredibly, people who go to the new-lows list when they're prospecting for stocks ignore the new-highs list, assuming that the stocks on that list are *too* high. In so doing, they decrease their chances of finding the next Linear Technology from "pretty good" to "almost nonexistent."

Another error that stems from the idea that strong stocks are not a good bet, and cuts seriously into investment results, is selling a winning stock too soon. Though this might seem a relatively minor problem, it actually can be very serious because it robs you of your really big profits—profits you need to offset the inevitable losses. It's in fact a bigger mistake than failing to cut your losses, because in a properly diversified portfolio the potential to profit from any one stock is far more than the potential of loss. That's just another way of saying that the most you can lose on a single stock is 100 percent of what you invested, but the potential gain is unlimited. If your objective is to make as much money as you can, *you must* put yourself in a position to hold onto really big winners when they come your way. If you have a system where you take the money and run every time you get a double or triple, eventually, and inevitably, you'll seriously shortchange yourself.

THINK BIG

The reason most investors fail to hold onto winners long enough is that they simply don't realize how big a move can sometimes be. They wrongly assume that if a stock has doubled or tripled, that's about the best they can hope for. However, investors who take the time to study the history of stock trends know better. Sometimes, a stock that has doubled will go on to make another tenfold increase. It can (usually does) take years for this type of move, but over a couple of years, your chances of riding a huge upward trend are far better than you'd think. The best way to convince yourself of this is to start studying long-term price charts of a broad cross section of stocks. The big movers are where you'll make serious money; not by calling it quits when things are going in your favor. The key to incredible profits is knowing how to keep from depleting your capital while you wait for the inevitable large winners.

FALLACY #5: CONTRARY THINKING IS THE WAY TO MAKE MONEY

Except at market extremes, the crowd is generally *right.* Contrarians, as understood by the popular definition of the term, are usually wrong, except at where the "crowd" has reached nearly unanimous consensus. When the crowd does agree unanimously about the direction of any market, the successful contrarian still takes no action until the market starts to confirm what he is expecting. This is the part of contrary thinking that most people do not understand.

The popular idea is that the contrarian investor is someone who is *always* doing the opposite of what most other people are doing. This understanding fosters tape fighting, and it brings disaster. Although sometimes it seems everyone wants to be thought of as a contrarian, in fact there are only small slivers of time when contrarians are right about the stock market—or anything else. The successful contrarian is highly selective about when to act against the crowd—and would never act against the market itself. Indiscriminate contrarians are trend-fighters, and over the long run trend-fighters seldom emerge with a profit.

It is much more profitable to be an independent thinker than to be a contrarian. An independent thinker sees things with more objectivity than the contrarian, who always wants to go against the crowd, whether or not the timing is right. The independent thinker has no axe to grind with the crowd but simply refuses to be influenced by it. Hence, the independent thinker acts contrary to the crowd only when clear thinking has evaporated and been replaced with irrational exuberance.

Although this discussion may sound academic, it isn't. Misunderstandings about what contrary thinking is and is not, contribute greatly to a tendency in investors to buy what is out of favor—and not yet far enough out of favor to be a good buy. Their decisions are out of synch with the market's trend. Generally they are too early—so early that they may lose tremendous amounts of capital waiting to be right. There is also the possibility that they will *never* be proved right. The *intelligent* contrary thinker, who is really just the independent thinker may observe irrational behavior in the marketplace, pushing certain types of assets to sky-high or ridiculously low levels, but, unlike the eternal or indiscriminate contrarian, waits to act until the market begins to confirm the accuracy of those observations. In other words, he waits for a trend to establish itself in the direction he is expecting.

Those who misunderstand the true, profitable meaning of contrary thinking are those who want to constantly be buying what is low and getting lower. After all, they have been told, by common folklore and by stories in business magazines, that the way to make money in the market is by contrary thinking. Eventually, most realize that there must be something wrong with their definition, but some never do understand. The moral of the story is, if you want to be a successful contrarian, question the common opinion but be aware of the market's direction at all times. Trends do not change direction in one day; the successful contrarian takes plenty of time to prepare for entering a contrary position while the trend is turning.

FALLACY #6: SUCCESS COMES FROM SETTING PRICE OBJECTIVES

A popular profit-limiting maneuver that has no place in the toolkit (or the mind) of the professional investor is the practice of setting *price objectives*. This is when you buy a stock and set a price where you will sell out if the stock reaches that target. These target prices are usually specified as a certain percentage above the entry price, but they may also be based on some analyst's assessment of the "value" of the stock.

However the target is arrived at, setting a target selling price is a seriously flawed practice, one closely related to the "what goes up must come down" belief. Anyone with significant investment experience can tell you that apparently overvalued items may continue moving much, much higher than anyone ever thought they could. The reason for this is quite logical: When a company's earnings are growing rapidly (or even just starting to do so), the price of the stock may be high relative to current earnings but may be only a few times the next year's *actual* earnings, *if next year's earnings could be known*. The stock may even be selling for many times the official earnings estimate for next year, because it takes time for good trends to be assimilated by stock analysts. Thus, the earnings projections of stock analysts tend to lag when something good is brewing (just as they often lag when bad things are in the works!). Just keep in mind that the aggregate consensus of all market participants (as reflected in the stock's price trend) tends to be more accurate and timelier than published earnings estimates.

If you study stock trends, you will come to the conclusion that the trend of a stock is a more accurate indicator of when to sell than any single person's calculated estimates of a stock's "value." Why, then, are price objectives used? They may be popular simply because retail brokerage houses and newsletter writers want to give some sort of selling advice to large numbers of retail clients. Price objectives make the task of giving advice to large numbers of people much more manageable. Unfortunately, it seldom results in the best possible outcome for a particular client. To be sure, the better brokers and advisers realize this and recommend more logical devices, such as trailing stop-orders to protect the downside while letting the stock price run upward as high as possible.

Target selling prices mostly just cap your profits, because once you sell you cannot possibly make *more profit* from that investment. Capping your profits is obviously not a good thing. If you employ a system that cuts your losses but also caps your gains, by definition you'll be worse off than if you had bought some stocks and done nothing but sit on them forever (assuming your portfolio was well diversified to begin with). Don't try to guess how far up a stock can move. If you do, you practically guarantee that you will never make substantial profits.

FALLACY #7: MARKET PREDICTION IS THE KEY TO PROFITABLE INVESTING

One widely held belief about investing in stocks is that in order to be successful, you must be able to predict the movements of the general averages in advance. Why do people assume this? Those who assume, mistakenly, that stocks bounce around in the same range forever, think they must predict market movements to be able to sell at the top of the range and buy at the bottom. For others, the desire to predict is borne out of human nature, which puts a premium on certainty. We love to know in advance what will happen. That is why the beginning investor thinks that being successful means becoming an expert at forecasting market trends. Experienced investors know better.

Some icons of Wall Street love to promote the importance of predicting the market because that's how they derive their livelihood. Others simply humor clients who are looking for market projections because it's easier to give them a projection than to try to correct their erroneous thinking. For instance, nearly every retail brokerage firm has a chief economist or market strategist whose main responsibility is to predict the climate for stocks. These firms recognize that in order to retain certain types of clients, they have to play the prediction game. (Of course, these firms almost always go with the odds and forecast a rising market— which also supports their retail sales operations.)

A large number of books and advisory services are concerned almost exclusively with predicting how the stock market in general will perform. Nevertheless, *the best way to make money in the stock market is to forget about predicting the future.* It's okay to hypothesize possible market scenarios, but to assume that you can tell in advance which scenario will play out is a fallacy. It only leads to investing during bear markets and other loss-generating behaviors.

Any serious review of what market gurus have said over a long period of time reveals a track record that is no better (and usually worse) than the average market return. There has never been a single person who has figured out how to predict the future of stocks—just as no one has been able to predict the future of politics. Though nearly all market advisors claim to be able to call major turns in the market, in fact every credible study ever done on the subject has proven all these claims false. Most market prognosticators significantly under perform the market, despite the universal claims to the contrary. Given the large number of market gurus, the laws of statistics suggest that *some* of them will be successful in predicting the market from time to time, but they lack the ability to repeat this performance continuously. The market beaters will usually be different for every time period that is sampled.

If the survey results are any indication, market forecasting appears to be prone to failure. The market spends about 60 percent of the time advancing, so if you just predicted an "up" day every day, you would beat most market prognosticators in the long run. Free yourself from the compulsion to predict the market.

This doesn't mean that you can ignore current market conditions, though. To be successful, you must always be aware of whether the market is bullish or bearish and adjust your actions accordingly. This book is designed to show you how to do this. But the basic message is this: Adjust your actions according to what is happening, not according to what is supposed to happen.

The key to success is to have a system for reacting to changes in market trends as they occur, one that ensures that our returns are as good as or better than the returns on the general market, whatever those returns may be. In other words, we need methods to keep in sync with the market's trend, because trends do persist for long periods of time. Having a system that keeps you out of the market once bearish conditions have been established is quite different from trying to predict when such conditions will occur.

FALLACY #8: GOOD INVESTORS ARE BORN, NOT MADE

After a number of bad experiences, many people, frustrated with their investment results, conclude wrongly that their personalities or intellects are missing some necessary attribute that would allow them to be more successful equity investors. In fact, it's what you think that determines your results: If there's something wrong with your results, it means you possess paradigms and dogmas about the stock market that are not true. Your challenge is to figure out what the incorrect dogmas are—and correct them.

INABILITY TO SEE THINGS CLEARLY IS AN ACQUIRED TRAIT

Show any five-year-old a series of stock charts and ask them which they would like to buy, and they will invariably choose the ones going up in price. Try it and see. As adults, though, we miss the obvious and simple truth that the child locks onto immediately. Perhaps we've gone to business school. Or maybe we've become successful in a career. We think we must know *something,* and that becomes our downfall. We adults look for complex analysis while missing the elementary truths.

Worse, what we think we know morphs into pride and ego. Once this happens, we not only miss the elementary truth that we should buy things that are going up, we start to imagine that we're smarter than the stock market itself. Proving that becomes the driver, rather than the quest for profits. We start to engage in self-destructive activities, like buying stocks that are sinking because our "analysis" says they shouldn't be sinking. What started as a simple pursuit of investment results can end in a cycle of pride, ego, loss, exhaustion, and, finally, frustration.

But it doesn't have to. The key is to let go of the idea that you know something. Once you do this, you can recover the ability to see the elementary truths that are so easily missed otherwise. Only then can you improve your results.

We all approach the stock market burdened down with preconceived but untrue notions that impede success. Your success as an investor will be determined by your ability to prioritize the elementary truths of the stock market and subordinate long-held dogmas to these truths.

FALLACY #9: THE STOCK MARKET IS A FORM OF GAMBLING

It's a tragedy when new investors lose large amounts of money and bitterly conclude that the stock market is just another form of gambling. This happens with every bear market, fostering beliefs that at their worst can lead to government meddling in free capital markets—something that is not necessarily positive for our country. Even a few highly educated types buy into this myth that investing in stocks is a form of gambling. More than once I've heard someone who was introduced as an "economist" say as much on a national news broadcast!

Investing and gambling are two totally different pursuits, and everyone who buys stock needs to know why. Once you realize the difference, it will give you confidence as you pursue a long-term plan for investing and will make you less prone to the destructive forces of fear and greed. Fear and greed do belong at the gaming tables; they don't belong in the stock market.

One prime reason to understand the difference between simple wagering and investing is that believing Wall Street is just a big gambling casino leads to self-destructive investing behavior. For some people, this is at the heart of their "take the money and run" philosophy, which they apply just as an investment is starting to pay off.

DIFFERENCES BETWEEN GAMBLING AND INVESTING

A share of common stock entitles the owner to a fraction of what is left over after all other stakeholders in a business have been paid. The firm takes in revenue from customers in return for its product and uses it revenue to pay for raw materials, employee wages, energy, supplies, and interest on borrowed funds. Anything left over belongs to holders of the firm's stock, who are essentially the owners of the firm. Depending on business conditions and how well the company is managed, what's left over can be very large, very small, or even negative.

Obviously, holders of common shares see more variability (risk) in what they take home than bondholders, raw material suppliers, or employees. The common shareholder stands last in line to be paid, and because this is a riskier position the shareholder demands a higher expected return than does the bondholder. In the stock market, investors are constantly trying to assess what will be left over for shareholders both now and in the future. That's why stock prices fluctuate, because business conditions are always changing, so what will be left over for the owners of a particular firm is always changing, too.

But one thing is for sure: Though common shareholders recognize that their returns may be volatile, they also expect that over the long run they will be *positive* and *permanent*—and higher than the return on bonds, Treasury bills, or other less risky investments. Despite fluctuations in value, the returns at some point should become permanent. And for as long as common stocks have existed (hundreds of years), this expectation has been met: Though stocks have had their ups and downs, and some very long dry periods, they have trended steadily higher in value. In fact, on average their value has increased faster than the value of dollars invested in more predictable vehicles like bonds or Treasury bills. Though recent bearish conditions may obscure that fact, it is indeed the long-term record. So, reality squares with economic theory in this case:— higher risk, higher return.

It is the steady upward progression in the value of stocks that really sets them apart from gambling. You could buy stocks, hold them for the rest of your life, and if your portfolio was truly well diversified, though the value might fluctuate over your lifetime, it's highly likely that they would greatly increase in value. Moreover, no other person would have *lost* money simply because your portfolio gained in value. This is not true with gambling, and it is the main feature that sets investing apart from gambling. In gambling, every dollar won is a dollar lost by someone else. It must be this way because gambling produces nothing, creates nothing, and therefore can only return to a winner what it took from a loser, minus the cut that goes to the house.

The value of common stocks increases without taking wealth away from anyone; in fact, when stock prices increase, the amount of aggregate wealth increases for society as a whole—the piece gets bigger. This is because common stockholders *do* produce something: They postpone the consumption of goods (i.e., they save some of their income) in order to supply the seed capital needed for businesses to buy equipment and produce goods. They get the ball rolling.

Here's another fact that highlights the vast differences between gambling and investing in stocks. With gambling, the longer you stay at the gaming tables, the more likely you are to walk away a loser. In the stock market, the longer you stay at it, the better chance you have of coming away a winner. In fact, if you buy and hold a well-diversified portfolio of stocks, you're virtually assured of making money eventually. Of course, many people do lose money in stocks, but only because they fritter their capital away with ill-founded trading strategies, fail to diversify, or fail to cut their losses.

Let me say that it's also true that without an investment plan that is well-founded and implemented with discipline, stock investing can surely seem like gambling in that it can be a way to lose an immense amount of money. During the past decade too many people succumbed to the idea that the rewards were great and the risks were small. Actually, the rewards are *commensurate* with the risks, nothing more, nothing less. There is no way to be absolutely sure of timing, so plans must allow for the possibility of bad timing, mistakes, and even the occasional foolish purchase. Investing without a plan is merely throwing money at the market, and history shows that this approach usually occurs at market highs, not market lows.

CHAPTER SUMMARY

We all approach the stock market with ingrained paradigms and fallacies that keep us from making good investment decisions. Certain widespread fallacies are the most common reasons why people can't change their thinking and get better results. Replacing long-held dogmas with accurate observations is the best way to change your thinking—which is the first step to changing your results for the better.

If you're not satisfied with your investment results, you're probably succumbing to one of the following logical traps, and have institutionalized one or more of these mistakes into your investment procedures:

1. You feel uneasy holding stocks that have made tremendous upward moves, so generally you take the money and run, thus systematically limiting your gains.

2. You gravitate toward stocks that are beaten-down and trending lower in price, thus systematically limiting yourself to poor-performing stocks.

3. You fail to set stop-loss orders for every stock purchase.

4. You have no loss-control plan for your portfolio of individual stocks.

5. You have no procedures for curtailing investments during bear markets.

These mistakes all stem from one or more of the fallacies discussed earlier in this chapter. To recover from them, diagnose which fallacies are driving you and eliminate them from your thinking. This book is intended to give you rules and procedures to replace every one of these hindering tendencies.

CHAPTER 7
TECHNICAL OR FUNDAMENTAL?

As I've said, some business school graduates emerge from their studies with the strong impression that the only way to build a profitable portfolio is by applying fundamental analysis techniques to the industry, the company's market position within the industry, its balance sheet, and so on. While as a student of finance I can see how this could happen, experience has shown me that these are not the only skill sets necessary to secure superior market returns. In fact, these may not even be the most important skills, because investment performance is determined by a combination of economic reality and investor psychology, and the relative effects of each are debatable. Typically, therefore, there is another education the graduate acquires after business school, learning through hard knocks that fundamental analysis, used in isolation, can lead to bad decisions.

Perhaps in reaction to the bad decisions fostered by fundamental analysis alone, there has long been a debate between investors focused on fundamentals and those who favor technical analysis of stocks based on their price action. Those who smugly dismiss technical analysis as black magic forget that it has a longer history than fundamental analysis (at least in the United States), because little financial data was required of publicly traded companies until the 1930s—which meant that the average investor had little real information to analyze. Those who embrace technical analysis, on the other hand, are forgetting the issues this lack of financial data brought on early in the twentieth century. Each approach has merits, and we should employ the strengths of each as we consider our own investments. However, as will become obvious as you read further,

I believe the market's opinion of a stock is more important than fundamental analysis using historical information.

One of the more useful aspects of financial analysis, and the one I favor, is the ability to detect and thus avoid the type of rich overvaluation problems witnessed during the Internet mania. Put another way, some quick checks of a company's valuation can help us understand *how much* risk we are assuming in our portfolio. And some fundamental data can help us to assess the *sustainability* of stock trends, whereas technical analysis can only show us their direction. Among the weaknesses of fundamental analysis is that, strictly adhered to, it can blind a person to developing opportunities. The market in terms of price trends provides the only up-to-the-minute data we have. Financial and fundamental data is typically old news, long assimilated by the market. Financial ratio analysis in particular can blind a person to growth opportunities; though these often carry a high price, they are also often well worth it. We'll discuss this in more detail in Chapter 8.

The main strength of technical investing, conversely, is the ability to quickly narrow down a list of potential investments to a select few, based on strong price trends; this is simply a summation of what the aggregate market thinks about a company's prospects. This market opinion is absolutely up-to-date, compared to the relative staleness of financial and fundamental data. If something good is happening to a company, it will show up in the price trend long before anyone outside the company or industry may ever be aware of it.

Another strength of technical analysis is that it allows a person to pick intelligent loss-limiting points, which, as you may already have realized, I'm convinced should be a key goal for all investors.

Of course, the weakness of using technical analysis alone is that it cannot detect when price and value have become grossly disconnected.

Without a doubt, this book emphasizes the technical approach far more than the fundamental approach. It is simple and effective, yet its value is enhanced when it is used with very basic fundamental analysis measures to help us avoid packing our portfolio full of hopelessly overvalued issues or issues that are all hype with no real value. Hence, we use the strengths of each approach to our advantage, without the academic debate over which approach is *more* right. If you're adept at intensive fundamental data analysis or have experience and insight into a particular industry, by all means use the entire range of your skills. Just don't let your fundamental analysis conclusions get too far out of sync with the market's assessment, as this is reflected in the price trend.

DO WE REALLY NEED TO VALIDATE THE MARKET'S OPINION?

Never forget this fact: It is *improving* conditions, not *perfect* conditions, which cause stock prices to appreciate. Today, many investment philosophies emphasize buying only stocks with perfect earnings growth, perfect return on equity, perfect margins, perfect this or that. Yet some of the best growth opportunities are represented by companies that haven't achieved perfection—yet—but do have highly competent management teams that are working toward that end. We can earn above-normal rates of return by assuming a little higher risk than "perfect" companies—but we must manage that risk via diversification, trading rules, and the other techniques introduced in later chapters. (By the way, sometimes a company with a perfect record may be riskier than those without perfect records—simply because expectations are so high that any disappointment can cause a run on the stock.)

The auction market that prices every stock every day gives us the best estimate by far of whether conditions for a company are improving or declining. Some of the best investments ever had spotty earnings records, appreciating many-fold before their earnings stream became "perfect." To have missed out on a stock with an outstanding price trend because of a spotty earnings record is a mistake. There have been too many times when I would have missed the boat on a double or triple if I had been looking for a perfect earnings trend or a perfect ratio analysis.

Is the market ever wrong, then? Absolutely. In this book, we try to minimize the possibility of choosing stocks whose prices are rising based on unsustainable conditions by applying the basic fundamental measures discussed in Chapter 8. The fact that the market is sometimes wrong is also the main reason we always place a sell-stop order immediately after buying *any* security, no matter how good we think our analysis or timing may be. This simple rule, adhered to without exception, will save you when the market has a fit of unwarranted optimism.

And what about professional fundamentals-oriented stock analysts? Are they ever wrong? Yes. They're in fact wrong far more often than the market is. Sometimes they're wrong because a stock's earnings trend and fundamentals become "perfect" just as the stock is peaking in price, while a stock that is early in an uptrend often has a less-than-perfect earnings history. Being seduced by company fundamentals that are improving while the stock price is rolling over is often what causes investors to *not* place a stop-loss, which can cause disaster. These investors are comforted by the conviction that their investment will come back up because of the research report they read. Often, it doesn't.

When you find someone fighting the tape like this, usually it turns out to be a fundamentals-oriented investor who has convictions about a "good company" with "great financials." Unfortunately, the fundamentals start declining only after the stock has already experienced a huge percentage loss in price.

CHAPTER SUMMARY

Because fundamental data is generally much older than the data coming from the auction market that is held every day on every stock, it should be subordinated to the market's opinion, which is future-oriented. The price trend neatly sums up the market's overall outlook for a stock (whether or not general market conditions are improving), without ambiguity or conflict of interest. No one analyst is smarter than the entire market.

To maximize profits, go with the market's opinion, do basic fundamental research to validate the sustainability of the apparent trend, and place a sell-stop just in case the market is wrong.

SECTION II
STOCK SELECTION

CHAPTER 8
PICKING STOCKS TO MINIMIZE LOSSES

GETTING THE BASICS RIGHT

If you are investing in stocks, you're looking for price growth, period. If the price of a stock grows enough, you probably won't care one bit about the firm's financial ratios. If you're looking for price growth, as a starting point why not measure price growth directly, in the trend of a stock, rather than measure things that may *influence* the price of the stock but don't take the whole picture into account? Statistics and financial measures may actually keep investors so busy that they never look up long enough to see the big picture.

The big picture can be seen readily by looking at the price chart of a stock. It's true, of course, that technical analysts can also be distracted from the big picture when they are distributed by certain indicators, oscillators, the convergence and divergence of market indexes, and other small-perspective approaches to analyzing a stock's every move. This type of technical analysis is not necessary to profit handsomely in stocks.

The reason many people do badly at investing is that they don't get the most relevant basics right. In the 80/20 world of investing, where 20 percent of the data determines 80 percent of the outcome, it's necessary to know what is *critical,* not merely interesting. If you can't make this distinction, you may profit, but not consistently. If you do make it, and concentrate on the top determining factors, you will do as well as anyone can expect to do.

In this section we will look at the criteria that are most important for picking stocks successfully and building your short-list of investment candidates. We'll get to the finesse points of entry and exit in a later chapter. The few basic technical and fundamental considerations that are most important are emphasized here. I'll show you how to focus on the really critical aspects of picking stocks, avoiding the losers (stocks that decline or do nothing) and stacking the odds in favor of your finding the winners.

DON'T BUY THE FAMILIAR

A word of caution: Many investors have subdued results because they gravitate to the names they know well. Personally, most of my really good picks over the years have been low-profile companies that, while great companies, were ones I hadn't heard of. Let the criteria discussed here lead you to the right stocks; *don't* start with a list of familiar, comfortable names and then try to apply these or other criteria.

TECHNICAL CONSIDERATIONS

TREND DETERMINATION

One very effective way to minimize the impact that the inevitable losses will have on your portfolio is to offset them with large-scale winners. Any study of price movements of individual stocks very quickly reveals that stocks make all price movements in trends.[1] These movements may be small, or huge. Given enough time, most stocks eventually have some noticeable price trends, unless they happen to be in highly defensive or mature-market industries.

Although most people know this, few take the time to realize its *implications.* As we've already discussed, one of the most common and foolhardy mistakes is to buy stocks simply because they're down. The common assumption is that if a stock has gone from 40 to 10, it's somehow more likely to get to 40 again than is a stock that has gone from four to 10. They are both at 10, but most novice investors assume the stock that's down in price will be a better bet than one trending upward. This is perfectly wrong. In fact, companies find it very hard to reverse trends, no matter which direction they're going. I know I've already mentioned this

---

[1] The composition of price trends is explored thoroughly in Chapter 13.

numerous times, but in my experience people need to hear it (and experience it with real money) many, many times before they change their bottom-fishing ways.

The shortest distance between two points, or two numbers, is a straight line. If a stock is destined to go from five to 500, of necessity it must pass through six, seven, eight, nine, 30, 50, 80, and 200 to get there. It does not have to pass through four, three, two, or one, although it may do so. This is one reason why picking stocks that are trending upward in price improves your chances of finding winning stocks.

If you were hitchhiking to a distant city, you would look for drivers who were going toward that city, correct? Why, then, do many investors look for stocks that have declined in price, rather than those whose prices are increasing? The reasons are strictly emotional: They "feel" safer buying a stock that once sold for a higher price; if they're ego-driven, they may want to look like a genius if they happen to buy the bottom. Over the years these falsely comforting approaches have led many investors to frustration or the poorhouse. They have no place in the mind of an investor.

Most investors will find it useful to study long-term charts to get a feel for how stocks make large price moves. Most of us need to learn through study just how far a trend can proceed. You can use the *Value Line Investment Survey* (found in most libraries) for this purpose, because its charts cover a long period and tend to show stocks that are doing well as well as those that are doing poorly. You can also use any number of free Internet chart services that are available to look at 10-year, 20-year, or even longer-term charts for stocks that started out unknown but are now well-known as blue chips.

As you study long-term charts, note just how many stocks have made 300 to 1,000 percent moves. It may be a revelation to you to know that this was true in both the bullish 1982-2000 period and in the 1970s, when the market was trapped in a large trading range for the entire decade. Such moves are not all that uncommon, and a few of them happen almost without interruption. Sometimes, stocks will even make more stunning moves of 2,000 to 3,000 percent over longer periods. It's almost inevitable that any stock in an uptrend will have periods of price correction, but there are some long trends where pullbacks do not exceed 30 percent to 50 percent of the stock's peak price.

Study the price chart of a stock that has had a large (four- to 10-fold) increase in price and note carefully just how many times the stock made a new all-time or at least a 52-week price high. The inference from this is something you may need to ponder: Someone who's *afraid* to buy and hold onto stocks making new highs if almost *guaranteed* to miss the benefits of large price moves. And yet, only by owning these very strong stocks can the true profit potential of stock investing be realized. Investors who dump shares once they get a good trend going may claim to want big gains, but their behavior dooms them to never achieve it. By studying how price trends occur, you will convince yourself to hold onto your winners rather than succumbing to the temptation to sell the winners to "lock in" profits. This is why your trading system and how you manage your stock picks are just as important as what you pick.

Finding good stocks with a strong upward trend is one thing, holding onto them is another. Both are necessary if you want to secure large gains.

MOMENTUM INVESTING

I anticipate that some readers will be skeptical about focusing on trending stocks because they've heard this described as "momentum" investing, something some investors sneer at as being dangerous or unsophisticated. Please understand that there is a world of difference between the foolish "momentum-only" investing that swept many neophyte technology investors out with the market tide in 2000 and what we encourage in this book. There is nothing wrong, and everything right, about using momentum as just one of our tools to find growth stocks.

In a sense, all investing is momentum investing. Who buys any investment unless there are hopes for a long upward trend to begin within a reasonable time? Then realize that it's much easier to observe a trend that's already begun than to anticipate one. That's why most successful investors buy where the market is in agreement with what they think should be happening.

Any stock with real potential for appreciation is by its nature somewhat speculative. I can say it no better than Wall Street icon Gerald Loeb: "There is no good investment which is not at the same time a good speculation."[2] This is true whether the investment is in buying real estate, stocks, or commodities. (Yes, I will concede that there are people who

---

[2] Gerald M. Loeb, *Your Battle for Stock Market Profits,* p.277. New York: Simon & Schuster, 1971.

buy real estate strictly for income, but the most successful real estate investors know that buying in an area of rising demand and rising prices is the way to make real money, even though they may sacrifice some current income to do so. Certainly, even income investors do not want their income offset by declining asset values.)

Using momentum to complement your investment toolbox is no more dangerous than any other form of investing—unless you fail to control losses. This is a key point. Upward trends do come to an end. Especially when the end is sooner rather than later, controlling the losses associated with trend-ending events is critical to your success. Momentum investing has acquired the reputation as being foolish and dangerous *only because it has been practiced by those who did not understand how to control the risks.* Most of these investors were so new to the market that they had never even been through one bear market cycle. By the time you finish reading this book, you will know how to assess, minimize, and control the risks associated with investing in individual stocks. Then, it will be up to you to discipline yourself to practice what you know.

The momentum approach and fundamental analysis of stocks are not mutually exclusive, although it has become common for people to think so. In stocks, you can use the trend while still digging further beneath the surface—and by all means, do so. You can't hurt yourself by knowing too much about the companies whose stocks you are thinking of buying. Yet I suggest that you restrict your list of companies to research to firms that currently are experiencing uptrends, ignoring do-nothing stocks. If you do, you will greatly skew the odds in your favor and avoid the temptation to buy stocks that are in the sick bay. In other words, combine the useful aspects of momentum, fundamental analysis, and risk control.

Though I was moderately invested in some technology and other momentum-based stocks when the bear market of 2000-2001 set in, I didn't get hurt very badly. The reason is not that I knew what was coming or was incredibly lucky. The reason is that I have simple but inviolable loss-limiting procedures in place. I always (and I mean, *always*) place a sell-stop order on any stock within a minute or two of buying it. I never lower the stop price after that, though I will raise it. We will deal later with a systematic plan for placing stop orders, but once again the entire point is to protect yourself from loss. Momentum investors aren't necessarily foolish, but momentum investors who aren't guided by a well-thought out plan for limiting their losses are foolish—and for the most part, poor.

Do Stock Trends Really Exist?

Any rational person is apt to ask this at some point. How can you really know that stock trends do exist, and persist?

To begin to respond, let's look at the aggregate Dow Jones Industrial Average (DJIA). From January 1, 1920 through December 31, 2001, there were 20,589 trading days. Of these, 1,809 were days when the average closed at the highest point it hit the previous year. On average, the three-month future return (i.e., the return for the three months after making the new high) for these trading days was 2.65 percent, or about 10.6 percent annualized. For all other days the three-month future return was 1.7 percent, or about 6.8 percent annualized. The 3.8 percent annualized difference in returns is significant enough to prove the point: Trends do have some value for indicating future returns, even in something as halting and slow-moving as a market average of fairly mature stocks like those in the Dow Jones-30 (DJ-30). Individual stocks in growing industries will tend to trend more than this average because in the long run both their risks and their returns are higher.

Table 8-1 shows five high-return stocks from the period between the market bottom on October 11, 1990 and December 29, 1995, with data on how their trends persisted during that time.

TABLE 8-1: Persistence of Trend

Company Name (Symbol)	Days on 52-Week Highs List (% of Total Trading Days)	First Appearance on New-Highs List	Split-Adjusted Price at First Appearance	Split-Adjusted Price on 12/29/95	Percentage Increase from First New High to 12/19/95
Ascential Software (ASCL)	126 (9.5%)	9/24/91	$0.99	$30.63	2,994%
American Vantage Co. (AVCS)	104 (7.9%)	5/3/91	$0.39	$7.32	1,777%
Educational Development Corp. (EDUC)	121 (9.2%)	10/10/91	$0.44	$10.88	2,373%
Glenayre Technologies (GEMS)	167 (12.7%)	10/11/90	$1.34	$41.69	3,011%
Prime Medical Corp. (PMSI)	205 (15.5%)	5/6/91	$0.50	$9.25	1,750%

There have been many exhaustive studies over the years proving that strong stocks outperform weaker ones in future periods, except during bear markets. But even during bear markets, the benefits of owning weaker stocks are deceiving. During bearish phases these studies are unfairly biased against the relatively strong stocks, because stocks that don't move up much, tend not to move down much, either, so the weaker stocks "outperform" by going nowhere during the bear market, just as they went nowhere when the market was rising. If you're going to assume the risk and effort of owning stocks, own stocks that have a good chance of moving up. Why buy stocks that have a history of doing nothing?

WHY STOCK TRENDS TEND TO PERSIST

If you still can't see the logic of restricting yourself to stocks that are currently trending upward, let me briefly explain why it makes sense that such trends will usually persist.

Some people erroneously believe that the only reason stocks keep trending is that more and more people are becoming aware of the company, and this ever-widening circle of buyers is the sole driver behind an increasing stock price. This is sometimes referred to as the "greater fool" theory, another phrase that some supposedly sophisticated investors, those who haven't really thought clearly about the subject, use to denigrate the use of simple concepts such as trends.

The actual reason why trends persist is that the trend reflects the reality of the business world. In the real world of business, companies that have superior management ability, technology, and the like do not acquire these competitive advantages overnight. It usually takes years of hard work, persistence, and targeted investment to build a company to the point that it can deliver superior returns to its shareholders. Then, once the competitive advantage is in place, it takes years for potential customers to realize that this company has a superior product or service to offer. As they do, the company's revenues and future outlook improve. This process is the real driver behind stock trends, and the notion that the stock rise is being driven simply by a gaggle of fools and even greater fools is founded neither in economic theory nor reality.

DETERMINING TREND DIRECTION

Determining the direction of a trend is simple and there is no reason to make it more complicated than it needs to be. Many services and publications do complex calculations to find things like relative strength, moving average crossovers, and the like, all to identify the trend. While these calculations are useful and there is nothing wrong with using them, they are not absolutely necessary for the investor assembling a pick-list of high-potential stocks. In addition to the relative strength rating published every weekday in *Investor's Business Daily* (as well as elsewhere), a stock is likely to be in an uptrend if any of the following are true:

1. The stock appears on the 52-week highs list published in almost any daily newspaper.

2. The stock is trading above its 50-day and 200-day moving averages.

3. The stock is trading above the price it was at six months and one year ago.

These are not the only ways of determining trend, and there is no hard and fast definition of exactly when an uptrend begins or ends, but they're a handy short-cut. If a stock fits even one of the above criteria, there is little doubt that its trend is up. At any given time there are hundreds or even thousands of stocks that meet at least one of the criteria, so you have little reason to look at stocks that don't meet them.

In this book, we concentrate on stocks whose prices are currently making 52-week highs, because the 52-week high list has a limited number of stocks appearing on it and it's also readily available and understandable. Most important, history demonstrates that all stocks making large moves spend a lot of time on this list.

WEEDING OUT CHOPPY OR THINLY-TRADED STOCKS

Once you have a list of stocks that are in uptrends, you next want to evaluate the day-to-day and week-to-week volatility of these issues. Stocks with choppy trading patterns may have one or more of the following problems:

1. Choppy stocks generally do not trend well, and we are looking for stocks that can trend upwards for a significant length of time.

2. A stock that has choppy price action may be highly leveraged.

3. These volatile issues may be in a precarious or declining industry or be affected by some other deterioration in quality having to do with the economy or their industry. Sometimes this situation is

betrayed in day-to-day volatility even before it shows up anywhere else, such as over the course of a long-term trend.

4. Getting in and out of volatile issues can be difficult, making it hard to limit your losses. This will also tend to reduce your portfolio ratio of winners to losers.

5. Extreme volatility can be a sign that a stock is thinly traded. Avoid stocks that trade less than 50,000 shares per day because the price spreads between bid and ask prices tend to be large, making entry and exit awkward and expensive.

In sum, what you want to be buying are stocks that have a history of making good-size trending moves but with minimal day-to-day volatility. While there are quantitative ways to check this, the quickest way is to simply review a stock's price chart[3] to determine whether it is likely to trend well. I recommend that you train your eyes to recognize smooth patterns that have good trending action without a lot of choppy day-to-day price swings. The evaluation is somewhat subjective but not overly so. Of course, no stock moves in perfectly smooth trajectories, yet some patterns are definitely better than others, as you'll see when you compare several stocks.

When looking for patterns, inspect charts that are both short-term (one year) and longer term (three to five years). Sometimes a stock that is making a new high looks choppy on the one-year chart but the three- to five-year chart reveals a different story. Figure 8-1 is an example of a stock chart that has a lot of volatility, but no discernable trend, despite the fact that it's at its 52-week high. The price swings in the trading range it is trapped in are absolutely huge, percentage wise, and it is getting nowhere. Technically speaking, the stock is in an uptrend, but I would avoid it for our purposes, based on the fact that it has a long history of not trending well.

---

[3]Most of the charts used throughout this book are *Japanese Candlestick* charts generated with the TeleChart 2000 program courtesy of Worden Brothers. Such charts convey includes more information than bar charts and are particularly useful for precision timing, a concept introduced later in this book. The long thin line represents the daily trading range for the day; the thicker center line represents the difference between opening and closing prices. On days where the price closes lower than it opened, the thick body of the figure is darkly shaded. When the closing price is higher than the opening price, the body of the figure is clear or lightly shaded.

FIGURE 8-1: NON-TRENDING SHORT-TERM STOCK CHART

The long-term chart for the same stock (Figure 8-2) also shows a long history of non-trending behavior. If a stock has gone three to five years with no sustained upward progress in price, chances are it is not going to zoom ahead anytime soon. There certainly are better propositions to be found.

Generally avoid issues trading fewer than 50,000 shares per day. There is no hard and fast rule about what defines "thinly traded," but the 50,000-share cutoff is pretty close to where it should be, especially if you need to buy or sell a large number of shares. On page 74 are charts typical of thinly-traded stocks, one a listed stock (Figure 8-3) and the other a

NASDAQ issue (Figure 8-4). Thinly-traded over-the-counter stocks have a different "look" to them than thinly-traded stocks on the NYSE or AMEX, primarily because the NYSE and AMEX have a specialist assigned to each stock who tries to create a continuous market. The absence of specialists on the NASDAQ market creates a much more haphazard look in the chart. The NASDAQ stock charted here, although it is at a new annual high in price, would be good to avoid because the market for it is fairly thin, as is apparent from the discontinuities in the daily trading patterns.

FIGURE 8-2: NON-TRENDING LONG-TERM STOCK CHART

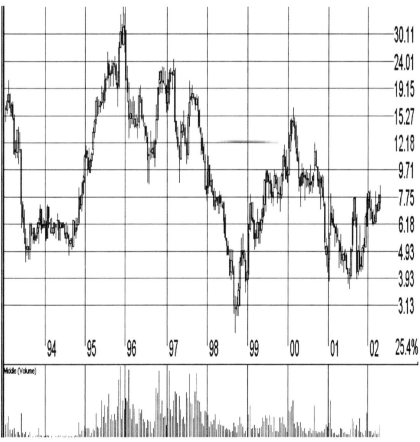

FIGURE 8-3: THINLY-TRADED STOCK: NYSE

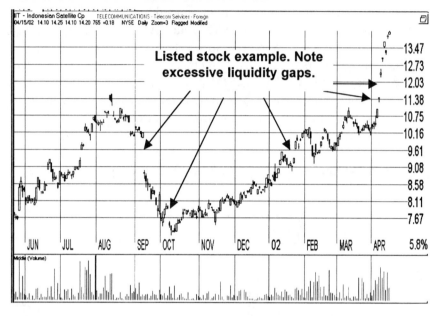

Listed stock example. Note excessive liquidity gaps.

FIGURE 8-4: THINLY-TRADED STOCK: NASDAQ

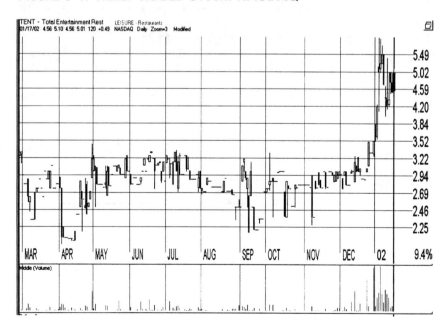

AVOIDING BEHEMOTHS AND DEFENSIVE ISSUES

All other things being equal, the growth potential of any company is inversely proportional to the following:

1. Annual sales or revenue volume

2. Market capitalization (number of shares outstanding x price per share)

3. Maturity of market or company's market share

Obviously, there is a tight correlation between all these things. Large-cap stocks are generally market-share leaders in their industry or have high annual sales volume. There are exceptions. During the Internet mania, for instance, we did see large capitalization paired with minimal revenue. That was an exceptional case—but even there a large market capitalization itself portended a limited upside for the investor.

The growth investor needs a compelling reason to invest in the very largest companies, because size alone can limit growth. The burden of proof is on the large-cap firm to make a case for why a growth investor should buy its stock. Compelling reasons could be, on the one hand, an exceptional business situation or, on the other, the investor's desire to diversify between small-, mid-, and large-cap stocks. In the latter case, I would argue that owning large-cap stocks is not really part of an aggressive growth system; it is a tactic for that part of your portfolio dedicated to moderate growth.

As an example, Microsoft may or may not turn out to be a decent investment going forward from 2002, when it was selling at 11 times sales revenue and 50 times trailing earnings, but it is certainly lower in growth *potential* than it was when it was one-tenth the size and sold for 50 times earnings. Reflecting the burden of size, the very largest stocks usually have a lower chance of developing a large price trend than do mid- and small-caps. When a company has a very high market share in its industry, it is hard to grow faster than the industry average because at that point, the company is the industry. For this reason, we should cross the largest, most mature companies off our list of potentials.

Where do we draw the line as to market capitalization? This is a moving target; what is considered large-cap today may be considered mid-cap, tomorrow. Today, in 2002, there is little doubt that a company with a of more than $100 billion is considered very much a large-cap.

Personally, I prefer companies capitalized at a maximum of $5 billion to $10 billion. The number you prefer will be influenced by your own degree of risk tolerance and your own thirst for growth.

Another set of stocks to cross off of our list is defensive issues, generally bought out of insecurity as investors seek safe harbors during bear markets. The stocks are called defensive because supposedly they defend the investor from loss; they are quite different from *defense* stocks, which are stocks of businesses that provide products or services used by the military. Defensive stocks have their day, but that day often ends as soon as a bull market begins. Here's an example: In 2001and 2002, real estate investment trusts (REITs) had an exceptionally good return after being driven up by yield-hungry dividend investors, especially considering that REITs are generally thought of as a conservative investment. As the market improves, these dividend-hungry investors (some of whom don't really understand what they're buying) may find out that REITs are not really so safe, because they stand a good chance of declining if interest rates climb.

Here are some issues and industries to avoid in an aggressive portfolio:

- Closed-end mutual funds (Stock and bond mutual funds trading as listed or OTC securities.)

- Supermarkets

- Preferred and convertible preferred stocks

- Gold mining stocks

- Banks and savings & loans

- Utility stocks (Though deregulation is turning this into a far less defensive industry.)

- REITs

- Stocks in "miscellaneous" or "unclassified" industries (These are excluded because they tend to be companies with an identity crisis—if your data provider doesn't even know what industry they are in, that's a clue that it may be wise to avoid them.)

There are periods when some of these groups offer tremendous returns, but they belong elsewhere in your portfolio, not in the aggressive growth portion that is what this book is mainly about. For instance, I always have some gold stocks in my portfolio, but as part of my overall asset allocation, not as a part of my aggressive portfolio of individual securities.[4] There are valid reasons for owning each of these groups of stocks, but growth is not one of them.

SPOTTING AND AVOIDING POST-BUYOUT COMPANIES

Avoid issues that are being traded publicly while the company is being acquired by another firm. These situations are easy to spot when you look at the stock chart, because there is generally a huge, sudden jump on heavy volume, with a corresponding gap in trading representing the point when the acquisition was announced; the example in Figure 8-5 is very typical.

FIGURE 8-5: STOCK CHART EXAMPLE OF A COMPANY ACQUISITION

---

[5]See Chapter 2 for portfolio allocation principles to protect yourself against long monetary cycles.

The reason to avoid this type of situation is that the stock's price movements will be limited until it is acquired and goes off the boards. You will be wasting time as well as money if you invest in it. If you have any doubt about whether a company is being acquired, check out the news on the Internet (*Yahoo! Finance* is good) to see if the company has announced any mergers or acquisitions.

DIVERSIFICATION AMONG INDUSTRY GROUPS

The reason for diversifying among several industry groups should be fairly obvious. Industry groupings are quite subjective matter; some data services break the universe of stocks into hundreds of disparate groups while others divide the same universe into only a few broad categories. No matter how you think of the universe of industries, make sure that your list of potential buys includes a variety of non-related industries. "Non-related" means industries that have little effect upon each other and that are not affected by the same external factors. During the recent technology mania, too many people learned the hard way that, for instance, diversification does not mean dividing your money between semiconductors, software, and computer wholesalers. Those who did "diversify" that way were rudely awakened as the tech sector began to melt away in 2000. The problem, of course, was that many people forgot that the technology sector is just that—a sector, not an entire economy. The NASDAQ 100 is essentially a sector-fund index, not a broad-based stock market index like the S&P 500 or even the Dow Jones Industrial Average. The Dow, while representing a very narrow set of 30 stocks, is far more broadly diversified (i.e., represents a far more diverse set of industries) than the NASDAQ 100 or the NASDAQ Composite index.

Even an actively managed aggressive growth portfolio needs to incorporate at least three radically different industries with relatively equal weightings of each. Five would be better. Some growth advocates recommend an extreme concentration of just a few stocks in one or two industries. If you did keep your selections that focused, you would certainly increase your potential return—and also your chance of a complete strikeout if a favored industry or company experienced a disaster or even just fell out of favor.

I sleep much better at night having 10 to 20 stocks in different industries than I would having just one or two. For a person who is good at picking stocks (as you will be if you use the criteria I recommend), having stocks in several industries gives not just a very good return but also peace of mind. In any bullish phase, there are always at least a handful of industries that lead the way, in the economy and in the market. One of the benefits of the past year or two of bearish activity has been to put to bed the neophyte's idea that two or three "good companies" are adequate diversification—especially if they're all in the same or highly related industries.

LOW-PRICED STOCKS

Low-priced stocks tend to be volatile and risky. Typically they're issued by small, unfounded companies or by companies that once had a higher share price but are now having a difficult time. They also tend to have a lot of day-to-day movement, sometimes without much forward progress. However, it would be less than impartial to altogether dismiss stocks with low share prices. The most astounding gainers do often come from the ranks of low-priced stocks—unfortunately, so do the largest decliners). For instance, Table 8-2 shows the average returns for the period March 6, 1991 to December 19, 1995, for the 10 largest gainers versus gainers in the 50-59 range and the 100-109 range. The March 6, 1991 to December 19, 1995 period was more typical of stock market movement than the 1995-2000 period.

TABLE 8-2: BEST PERFORMING STOCKS, MARCH 6, 1991-DECEMBER 19, 1995

	Average Return over the Period	Average Opening Share Price
Top 10 Gainers	3,197%	$0.77
Gainers 50-59	977%	$3.91
Gainers 100-109	670%	$5.38

The largest percentage gainers consistently come from the universe of lowest-price shares. The correlation between return and beginning share price is fairly consistent. It also squares with economic theory nicely, in that it is not surprising that less-established, riskier companies offer the potential for higher, though less predictable returns.

That's the good news about low-priced shares. But the problems are huge. The main one is that the failure rate of companies in this price range is high, meaning you have to own several times the usual number of companies in a category to be anywhere near assured of having enough winners to more than offset the many losers. In other words, you'd have to pick 20 to 30 low-priced stocks from the new-highs list to get adequate diversification. Even then, if your timing were bad, the portfolio may go down. The market can sometimes be cruel to these types of stocks.

Please recognize that Table 8-2 shows low beginning share prices for the largest gainers during the period studied, it does *not* suggest that the average return of stocks in that price range would be anything like these. The table excludes the losers, and includes only the largest winners in the universe of low-priced stocks. The number of losers relative to the number of winners was undoubtedly substantial. If you happen to lock onto the right low-priced stock, the rewards can clearly be tremendous. There's no way around the fact that they can provide a good return under the right circumstances, but finding the right circumstances is crucial.

The trading patterns of stocks under $5 per share are especially erratic and the attrition rate is extremely high. Moreover, most stocks under $5 are not marginable. They also tend to have liquidity problems.

I see nothing wrong with including some shares priced between $5 and $15 per share in your portfolio, given their potential. Just don't get carried away. Concentrate the vast majority (at least 80 percent) of your individual stock purchases in companies selling for more than $15, and preferably at least $30. You'll find plenty of room for growth, and the trading patterns in that price range are much more predictable.

AVOIDING OVERBOUGHT SITUATIONS

It's always very unpleasant to buy a stock and run into an immediate, nasty correction. Even worse is when you buy a stock and it declines to hit your sell point within a matter of a few days. To lessen this probability (although there's no way to eliminate it), we need an additional filter. On any given day, there are perhaps a few dozen to a few hundred stocks making it onto the new-high list. Of these, a certain percentage would be poised for an abrupt reversal. When a stock becomes overextended—when it has run up "too far, too fast"—it has to give back some of that gain even if it will eventually head higher. Those with "weak hands" (short-term investors, especially) will sell the stock to lock in some quick profits. This selling can feed upon itself, resulting in a quick, hopefully short sell-off that, if market conditions are favorable, will be less than the previous run-up in price. Generally, the downward reversal is at least as fast as the preceding rally, because the purpose of the correction is to scare the weak holders out of the stock. The weakest holders are those who have no system to rely on for decision-making but are simply buying and selling on emotional impulse.

To avoid getting hit with immediate corrections, keep an eye on the 50-day moving average (MA) for the stocks that are on your buy list. In general, avoid stocks making new highs that are more than 25 percent above their 50-day moving averages. In other words, if a stock's 50-day MA is $20, don't spend any more than $25 on the stock, because 125 percent of $20 is $25. If the stock you're looking at is more than 25 percent above its 50-day, move on to another stock. There is almost always something making a new high that is within this range; if there isn't, it may be that the entire market is overbought. For your entry point, look for that "sweet spot"—a new high in a situation that's not overbought.

The 50-day MA for any stock can be found easily in this age of information. *Yahoo! Finance,* for instance, has charts of 50- and 200-day MAs. Another excellent resource is *StockCharts.com,* one of the few places I've found that delivers the actual 50-day MA value.

Please note: As with most things, there's nothing magical about that 25 percent number. Still, the concept is sound: The higher a stock is above its 50-day MA, the more susceptible it is to a pullback. My own feeling is that 25 percent represents about the maximum amount above the MA that I might be willing to pay.

FUNDAMENTAL CONSIDERATIONS

CONFIRMING FACTORS

Just about every stock that is trending upward has improving earnings. However, not every stock trend has staying power. While the stock's trend is as trustworthy as anything we can find to indicate an improvement in the company's outlook, what we need is a simple way to increase our odds of picking companies where the trend is likely to continue.

Earnings growth alone is nice but it says little about staying power of a trend, for these reasons:

1. Earnings are easily manipulated.

2. If you know anything about accounting, you know that the very concept of earnings is highly theoretical. For that very reason the Financial Accounting Standards Board spends much of its time trying to clarify how to match revenues and expenses.

3. Earnings are also quite volatile; a wide variety of short-term factors can push them up or down for a quarter or two.

For assessing the sustainability of a trend, cash flow is not much better. Typically, it's calculated by taking reported earnings and adding back non-cash expenses like depreciation. Since the starting point for calculating cash flow is earnings, it's subject to virtually the same problems as those of earnings themselves.

Sales growth, on the other hand, is a superior tool for determining trend sustainability, for the following reasons:

1. In most industries, revenues are far less volatile than earnings. Because the relative merits of competitors' products do not change overnight, we seldom see a situation where customers switch suppliers en masse, even in consumer industries. A company generally loses market share to another quite gradually, so recent sales trends tend not to turn stale nearly as quickly as other reported data.

2. Sales and revenues are not easily manipulated to inflate reported results. Sales are real and measurable. Usually, they refer to products actually billed and shipped for the reporting period. Companies trying to "improve" reported results seldom play with the sales line of the income statement; they play with the lines *below* the sales line.

3. Earnings growth without sales growth is generally not sustainable.

4. Sales growth is probably the best, most reliable indicator of whether the company's value proposition is attractive to customers. It's even better than surveying potential customers because it tells us what they are doing, not what they say they will do.

SALES GROWTH

Without sales growth, long-term earnings improvement is nearly impossible. On the other hand—gross mismanagement excepted—sales growth almost always results, sooner or later, in earnings improvement. The earnings improvement may at first be simply a narrower loss than was previously experienced, but a narrower loss is the precursor to profits. Hence, a narrower loss can be the beginning of a positive price trend for the stock, even before earnings materialize. Take the time to check sales growth because sales are the engine driving earnings. Like an automobile whose engine has died, a company without sales growth may be able to coast on earnings for a while by emptying built-up expense reserves and such, but without sales growth, earnings will eventually stop moving. When a company is growing earnings without growing sales, there is a greater chance of either "creative" accounting or that the trend in earnings is not sustainable. Because reported sales are not easily manipulated, they tend to be more "real" than earnings anyway and give a better picture of the real demand for a company's products.

So validate that sales are growing at some acceptable rate of growth—the higher, the better, but I would certainly like to see at least double-digit sales growth in the most recent year.

How do you use sales growth as a stock selection criterion? For each company I'm considering I like to multiply one-year sales growth rates by one-year share price growth to obtain a growth factor.

This is an indicator of market trend strength and trend sustainability; it gives us a quick snapshot of both the market trend and whether the company has a confirming underlying increase in sales. Used as a ranking device, it ensures that we invest in stocks with the best market (price) performance and demonstrated sustainable product attractiveness.

FINANCIAL RATIO ANALYSIS FOR STOCK SELECTION

I would caution you against going overboard on screening out stocks based on financial ratios and valuation measures. To paraphrase the earlier quotation from Gerald Loeb, "If a stock is not a good speculation, it may turn out to be a poor investment." Financial ratios measure only what has happened in the past, and the economy is highly dynamic. Companies' fortunes change faster than ever before. Most stocks with growing sales, earnings, and share prices sell for one-and-a-half to two times the P/E ratio of the average stock—as they should. Some sell for even more, especially those issued by smaller companies with a tremendous competitive advantage and a lot of room for growth. So where do we draw the line on valuations? The objective and correct answer is, *we don't draw the line.*

Financial data and ratios tell you nothing about a company's ability to generate income in the future, which is the prime determinant of value for any investment. History clearly shows that most of the companies offering the best returns come from the ranks of moderately "overvalued" stocks, and not just during the abnormal 1990s! Resign yourself to the fact that many high-potential stocks are not going to have low P/E or low price-to-book-value ratios. This is because traditional measures of a stock's value generally are of little use in circumstances where earnings are growing very quickly. One of the worst things we can do to ourselves as investors is to cling to screening criteria that virtually guarantee that we will avoid the biggest gainers.

Investors who use financial measures as stock selection criteria are often misled into buying stocks that are declining in price. Here, I would like to briefly review some popular financial ratios that investors commonly use to make decisions, and the practical problems with each.

PRICE/EARNINGS (P/E) RATIO

The only thing a low P/E ratio tells us is that the stock is selling for a low price relative to the previous year's earnings. It doesn't tell us whether that years' earnings were unusually high or low, whether the company is growing or will grow in the future, etc. Using P/E ratios to determine the attractiveness of an investment is based on a naive, static view of the world. It's like using last month's weather forecast to schedule this month's picnic: It's not so much that the information is inaccurate, it's just too dated and too limited to be of much use.

Beginners believe that a stock that's selling at a low P/E ratio must increase in value. This approach to selecting stocks is flawed because it assumes all companies have roughly the same prospects for future earnings growth. But the reality is that companies have vastly different outlooks for growing earnings and that's why the market rightly assigns a low P/E ratio to some stocks and a high one to others. Some companies grow earnings at two to three percent per year for years and years on end. Other companies grow earnings at 20 to 30 percent per year for years and years on end. It's absurd to assume, as proponents of a low-P/E ratio system do, that a company is positioned for high growth should be priced the same as a stodgy company in a mature industry.

PRICE/BOOK VALUE (P/BV) RATIO

Another popular but flawed concept that leads investors into buying stocks that are declining is the practice of buying stocks that are selling for a low price relative to book value (P/BV). Book value is calculated by taking the historical (not current) value of the assets owned by the firm and subtracting any debts or other liabilities the firm may have.

There are three problems with using this calculation as an investment screening parameter:

1. Book values as calculated by accountants often bear no resemblance to the real value of assets on the balance sheet.

2. Shares that are selling for a low P/BV are doing so for a very good reason: These firms invariably earn a very low return on their assets. In fact, the value of a firm's assets does not matter; what matters is what the firm can earn for its shareholders. A person looking for low prices relative to book value forgets most firms earning substandard returns on their assets will generally keep on doing so.

3. Most of the earning power of a firm is determined not by physical or financial assets but by the abilities of the people working for it (human capital) and by the reputation and position of the firm in the market it serves. Because book values capture none of this, they thus ignore completely the most critical assets a firm possesses.

RETURN ON EQUITY (ROE) PERCENTAGE

More and more, it seems, I hear someone suggest that return on equity is somehow the way to tell a good investment from a bad one. Aside from the obvious problem that ratio may simply be telling us that a firm is over leveraged (too little equity, too much debt), there are other problems with it. The main one is that it's just a by-product of the P/E and P/BV ratios, as follows:

$$ROE \text{ (percent)} = \text{Earnings} \div \text{Book Value}$$

Therefore;

$$ROE \text{ (percent)} = (E/P) \times (P/BV)$$

Where:

E = Earnings per share (EPS)
P = Share price
BV = Book value per share

Because it's just a by-product of the P/E and P/BV ratios, ROE is subject to the limitations of each that I've already mentioned. This highly popular but somewhat misleading ratio tells us what the shareholders' current return would be if they were investing money (i.e., buying the company's stock) at exactly a 1:1 price to book value per share. One of the problems with ROE is that these days we usually pay far more than that. However, the major problems are the ones associated with the P/E and P/BV ratios themselves.

Many people labor under the delusion that if they buy a company with a high ROE, say 25 percent, then somehow they are buying this current return for *themselves*. This is most certainly not true. When the ROE calculation came into common use in the mid-20th century, few companies sold for many times their book value. They do now. Then, ROE was elegantly simple to calculate, and useful at the same time—it did roughly reflect the return available to the public investor. Since few good growth companies these days sell for a P/BV of one or less, we need to understand that the return we are buying is less than this.

Many investors these days comfort themselves when they pay 100 times earnings by looking at ROE. A company may indeed be worth 100 times earnings, but not simply because it sports a high ROE. If a stock fits our selection criteria, buy it. But don't buy a stock simply because it has a high ROE, and don't pass on one because it has a low ROE, either.

In the 2001-2002 season I had several doubles, despite a nasty bear market and subdued, very selective, investment activity on my part. The ROE for four of the best were: 9 percent, 12 percent, 13 percent, and 80 percent. Had I been focused on ROE as a selection measure, I would probably never have bought three of the four stocks that ultimately doubled in price. Again, *improving* results, not *perfect* results, are what makes for an appreciating stock.

The stock's price trend tells us whether the situation is improving or getting worse. Do we think our accounting skills are better than the market's assessment? Do we really need to double-check the entire market's assessment by letting a financial ratio drive our investment activity? Of course not. The market's assessment is more accurate than our personal evaluation of an accounting measure, no matter how skillful we may think we are at that kind of analysis. ROE, like most financial measures, is also of limited usefulness in choosing stocks for investment. Don't avoid buying a stock just because it has perfect results (if your analysis says that), but don't think these are the only stocks worth buying, either. Stick to stocks with a good price trend and strong sales growth—if you do, perfect financials are superfluous.

FINANCIAL RATIOS IN GENERAL

These three ratios are not by any means the only metrics investors use to make decisions, but they are probably the most widespread, persistent, and limiting. Because of their limitations it is best to avoid stocks that are declining in price, even if financial measures appear to make them good values. If you are a growth investor, you don't begin your search for winning stocks by screening for low-P/E issues, low P/BV issues, and the like. Experienced business managers aren't attracted to ailing companies' shares, because they know firsthand how difficult it is to reverse the fortunes of a failing or lackluster firm.

That said, I must mention that it is also a mistake to avoid low-P/E stocks simply because they are low-P/E stocks. Sometimes low-P/E issues are in favor; this often happens after bear markets as people slowly regain their courage to venture back into equities. Later on, when the bull market is in full swing, these issues may take a back seat. If the criteria in this section lead you to a low-P/E stock, buy it. That's quite different from limiting yourself to stocks with low valuation ratios. If a low-P/E stock is trending upward, there's no reason not to buy it unless it has a long history of not moving much—if it does, it probably won't move much this time, either.

HOW SHOULD A GROWTH INVESTOR USE FINANCIAL MEASURES?

There is a proper way to use accounting data, but it's not to pick stocks. It may be useful for telling us when we are unwittingly assuming too much risk. It's best to have a balance of risk within your portfolio, so if you had been sitting in 1999 with 100 percent of your money invested in dot-coms with no sales or earnings, you would want to be reminded of that. The lesson is that we should monitor how much risk is in our portfolio at all times, and then manage the risk with capital preservation techniques.

MOST GOOD STOCKS HAVE SOME AIR IN THEM

Because valuation levels of certain equities have increased tremendously over the past 20 years, we do need some way of protecting ourselves from filling our portfolio with good companies selling at absolutely awful prices. For this, I propose a very simple metric: the price-to-sales (P/S) ratio. Having just written about the dangers of using the P/E and other ratios to pick stocks, this may sound contradictory, but it isn't, for this reason: We will use this ratio as a last step, to assess whether we have a balanced risk level in our portfolio, not to screen or find stocks. Though financial measures aren't useful for picking stocks, they can keep us from devoting too large a percentage of our assets to the most optimistically valued equities and can help us better understand how much risk we are taking.

Instead of laying down a wise-sounding but foolish dictum like "Never buy stocks with a P/E higher than 50," I would just encourage you to review the P/S ratio of the stocks on your buy list to find ones that may be extreme "outliers" in terms of valuation. At this writing, 6,432 of the most actively traded stocks have the distribution shown in Table 8-3.

TABLE 8-3: PRICE/SALES RATIO DISTRIBUTION FOR ACTIVELY TRADED STOCKS

Price/Sales Ratio	Number of Companies Selling at This Price (Percentage)
Between 0 and 4.99 times sales	5,541 (86.2%)
Between 5 and 9.99 times sales	471 (7.3%)
Between 10 and 24.99 times sales	232 (3.6%)
25 times sales or greater:	188 (2.9%)

Only 188 stocks have a price/sales ratio of 25 times or greater. A quick check of their charts shows that very few of them are showing strong uptrends, so the reason they're selling at high valuations is not because they're world-beaters or possess breakthrough technology. (Though among these there certainly are *some* companies with strong uptrends that may be well worth considering.)

You need to apply some common sense here. For instance, I would be less concerned about a price/sales ratio of 25 for a still-developing biotechnology company than for an auto manufacturer. However, for the sake of discussion, let's assume 80 percent of my portfolio was composed of stocks sporting a P/S ratio greater than five (that is, the top 10 to 15 percentile rank in terms of valuation). This discovery would certainly give me pause. It would probably cause me to rebalance things by trading some of these in for issues with an equally strong share price growth trend and sales growth trend but valued more conservatively relative to sales. You would never want to buy a stock that was trending downward, no matter how low its price/sales ratio, but holding a preponderance of extremely high P/S ratio stocks may be a tip-off to overly optimistic expectations.

WHY USE THE PRICE-TO-SALES RATIO?

When screening for potentially excessive valuations, use the price-to-sales ratio because:

1. At any given point, any company worth investing in has revenues. Many, many good developing or cyclical companies go through periods where they have negative earnings and therefore no P/E ratio. Because the P/S ratio can be calculated for just about any firm,[5] it represents a basis for gauging how optimistically-valued the stock is in relation to other stocks.

2. Reported *earnings* are easily manipulated by company management. Revenues *can* be manipulated, but this is very rare and is generally fraudulent or illegal when it is done. Put another way: Sales are real, earnings are theoretical. If you don't believe me, ask any accountant.

---

[5] P/S ratios are not technically computable for banks and thrift institutions, but we are not considering these somewhat defensive issues for the aggressive portion of our portfolio.

Naturally, you can expect that growing industries will have higher price/sales ratios than cyclical or low-growth industries. Don't be afraid to hold some stocks with a higher P/S ratio, but not too many.

CHECK THE NEWS

Before you buy any stock, check the news about the company. Avoid situations where another firm is acquiring the company, because, though the chart of such a firm will probably look great, the upside is almost always limited once the acquisition has been announced. Also, avoid situations where the company's entire outlook hinges on a single outcome. The classic case is the one-drug wonder firm. If the drug has promising test results or a favorable FDA ruling, the stock soars, but if the outcome is unfavorable, there is a significant overnight gap to the downside. Neither of these situations lends themselves to steady, rapid appreciation, which is what we want from our stocks. The single outcome company is probably the closest thing to gambling the stock market has to offer.

EXCESSIVE SCREENING CRITERIA CAN HURT YOUR RESULTS

When using screening programs to select stocks for maximum investment gains, please question the popular assumption that the more criteria you use, the better. In fact, the opposite may be true. Here's a real-life example of how applying successive layers of screening criteria can actually *exclude* the best gainers from your portfolio. On April 30, 2002, the stocks shown in Table 8-4 ranked as having had the best one-year percentage returns.[6]

The following popular screening criteria would have eliminated these from the consideration of an investor doing his prospecting in early May 2001:

1. A *Low-P/E screen* would have eliminated all but two (lines six and seven) from consideration.

2 A *High Current ROE percent screen (ROE >15 percent)* would have eliminated all but possibly line seven (TSA).

3 A *High Long-Term ROE screen (5-year ROE >15 percent)* would have eliminated all.

[6]Stocks selling for less than $10 at the end of the period were excluded. Otherwise, the largest percentage gainers would have been more substantial. Also, these were the top gainers for which historical information was available at the time of writing.

4. *Positive 1-Year Sales Growth* would have eliminated lines five and seven.

TABLE 8-4: SCREENING CRITERIA AND ONE-YEAR RETURNS[7]

Line Number	Ticker Symbol	1-Year Return	1-Year Sales Growth	5-Year Sales Growth	1-Year ROE	5-Year Average ROE	P/E Ratio
1	HGR	1,109%	+40%	+50%	-9%	1%	NM
2	INVN	736%	+36%	+31%	-4%	12%	NM
3	HLYW	607%	+18%	+35%	NM	N/A	NM
4	APTM	572%	+98%	-9%	-70%	-370%	NM
5	BLUD	523%	-13%	+17%	NM	0%	NM
6	MOVI	505%	+15%	+8%	+7%	1%	6
7	TSA	440%	0%	2%	+18%	-17%	11

Any combination of the criteria would most likely have eliminated all of what were destined to be top performers. These stocks were not cherry-picked to skew the results, though this is admittedly far from an exhaustive study. Nevertheless, it does illustrate the principle that trying to buy into seemingly risk-free opportunities can eliminate upside potential as well as downside. This should hardly be a surprise to those who understand the relationship between market risk and reward. It is much better to *manage* risk than try to avoid it altogether.

Since huge gainers tend to come from the ranks of low-priced shares, all the stocks charted were low-priced (less than $10) shares at the beginning of the one-year period measured. There will no doubt be criticism that they are somehow not "representative" of investment-grade (whatever that means) companies. Here is a similar list for the same period, but with only higher-priced shares represented. These companies shown in Table 8-5 were the top gainers for the universe of stocks that closed above $30 per share on May 1, 2002. These stocks started the year at prices ranging from $8.50 to $15.20.

---

[7]One-year sales growth, one-year ROE percent, and P/E ratio approximate readings available at the beginning of the period of time studied (May 2001). Calculations derived from data obtained via EDGAR Online. Five-year averages are current as of the end of April 2002. *Source:* Multex Investor.

TABLE 8-5 TOP GAINERS, MAY 1, 2002

Line Number	Ticker Symbol	1-Year Return	1-Year Sales Growth	5-Year Sales Growth	1-Year ROE	5-Year ROE	P/E Ratio
1	ACMR	386%	17%	25%	10%	12%	10
2	ASCA	268%	14%	27%	-120%	-7%	NM
3	SAH	243%	81%	76%	16%	15%	6
4	TSCO	238%	10%	13%	11%	13%	8
5	CHTT	204%	-15%	11%	-4%	73%	NM
6	GRTS	202%	10 %	33%	26%	4%	4

As you'd expect with higher-priced shares, the financial ratios of these companies were better than the ratios for the companies shown in Table 8-4, but they're still far from the best ratios out there. In other words, these were also not perfect companies from a financial performance standpoint. Only one had a current ROE higher than 20 percent, a common screening criterion these days—and one that would have guaranteed that the person using it would have avoided almost all of these, the largest winners of the year.

Note that most stocks in both lists had impressive one-year sales growth and spent most of the year in solid uptrends.

The only intent here is to show that a process many investors employ (multiple-criteria screening using financial ratios) can actually work against strong investment returns. The lesson, in my opinion, is this: If you're going to use multiple criteria, you'd better make sure they're criteria that actually increase the likelihood of finding large percentage gainers. Don't rely on common assumptions about financial ratios having predictive value. It's simply not true that there's no harm done by using lots of popular but irrelevant criteria, as we have seen.

The two lists also illustrate another point. Most of the stocks on them were far from "perfect" in terms of financial performance when they began increasing greatly in value. Once again, it's *improving* performance, not perfect performance, which increases stock prices. Limiting yourself to stocks with pretty ratios and razor-straight earnings growth curves can foster a feeling of comfort, because those companies are viewed as less risky. Probably they are. But the other side of the economic law of risk and reward is this: *By eliminating risk, we may also eliminate opportunity.*

To buy stocks, perfect or imperfect, without a loss-limiting plan for controlling risk would be foolish, but there's a fine line between assuming risk while controlling it via diversification and loss-cutting rules and avoiding risk altogether. It's like the difference between investing in certificates of deposit and investing in equity mutual funds. It's easy to see that no one ever got rich by avoiding risk by investing in CDs. To get superior returns, you have to embrace risk, but manage it. To make big gains without taking 50 years to produce them, we need to be willing to stick to just a few criteria that actually stack the odds in our favor, and be willing to include some less-than-perfect stocks in our portfolio. This is why I have tried to stick to only the bare minimum criteria necessary to find improving companies.

CHAPTER SUMMARY

The first step in choosing stocks for investment is to get the big picture. No matter what you do after that, you cannot succeed unless you prioritize the most essential criteria. These criteria are:

1. *Get the trend right.* Only buy stocks that are increasing in value. The simplest and fastest way to find these is on the listing of new 52-week highs from your favorite newspaper or other source. Take this as your beginning point and narrow the list from there. The market votes every day on which companies are doing well, and the market's best estimate is certainly better than any analyst's.

2. *Eliminate excessively choppy or thinly traded securities.* Look at bar charts of stock trading patterns. Avoid stocks trading less than 50,000 shares per day.

3. Eliminate the very largest of large-capitalization issues. Their growth potential is limited. Also eliminate defensive issues like closed-end funds, grocery stocks, and REITs.

4. *Eliminate stocks that may be going off the boards soon.* Check the news pages to see if a buyout or merger is in progress.

5. *Diversify between unrelated industries.* Try to have three to five industry groups represented in your selections.

6. *Limit stocks trading less than $15 per share to less than 20 percent of your holdings.* Avoid stocks costing less than $5 a share altogether.

7. *Avoid grossly overbought situations.* Eliminate from consideration stocks trading for more than 25 percent above the 50-day moving average price.

8. *Calculate the growth factor for each candidate stock.* Multiply the one-year sales growth percentage by the one-year share growth percentage. Use this both to rank market strength and confirm the sales trend.

9. *Do a quick check of the price-to-sales ratio.* Make sure the majority of your selections are not on the outer extremes of optimistic valuations. It's all right to have some stocks with high P/S ratios, but not all. Strike a balance in your selections.

10. *Check the news headlines for your stocks, online.* Look for relative unknowns that may be affecting the stock price.

CHAPTER 9
PRACTICAL APPLICATION OF STOCK-PICKING CRITERIA

In this chapter we will pick a set of 10 high-potential stocks for addition to a portfolio using the criteria just discussed. The mechanics I will walk you through are not by any means the only way to get the necessary data or apply the criteria. For the sake of clarity, I've concentrated on doing the research in this example manually, using easy to find and inexpensive data sources. That means some number-crunching will be required. In reality, free or subscription-based data services are readily available on the Internet, and this entire process can be accomplished with much less time and effort, but I think the illustration is clearer if we do it the hard way.

Later in this chapter, I also present an alternative, less manual, and less-time-consuming example using free, online tools as a beginning point.

Since the criteria discussed in Chapter 8 are screening filters, they can be applied in any order without affecting the results. In other words, though the criteria are applied in a particular order in this example, there's nothing special about the sequence.

AN IMPORTANT CAUTION

The sample portfolios selected in this chapter are derived using data current as of the time of this writing, April 2002. It's a bear market right now. In Chapter 12, I present trading rules designed to keep you from selecting stocks during bear markets. The reason is that stock selection techniques in general don't work well during bear markets, and the ones I present here are no exception. In bear markets, stocks in solid uptrends quickly turn to stocks in solid downtrends. Buy stocks only when the market environment supports increasing stock prices. In April 2002, the stock market in the U.S. was definitely in the throes of a severe bear market as defined in Trading Rule Number Four (Chapter 12). Hence, in a real-life, real-money situation, an investor following the trading plans presented later in this book would have no business (almost literally) selecting a portfolio of stocks at a time like this. But since I'm not putting any real money in the market for this example, I'll go ahead.

Keeping this important point in mind, the sample portfolio selections in this chapter should be viewed only as examples presented for training purposes. These examples walk you through the steps you would take to select a portfolio of high-potential stocks when market conditions are favorable. When Trading Rule Number Four tells you that you are in a bear market, move to the sidelines where you can watch other people getting bloodied by equity investments.

NEW 52-WEEK HIGH FILTER

Our starting point in building a portfolio is to find a list of stocks that are making new price highs relative to the past year. These are all likely to be in the midst of upward price trends, our most important criterion. I'm using yesterday's *Investor's Business Daily* (*IBD*, available for $1.25 at almost any newsstand) as my source for a new-highs list. This would be the Monday, April 22, 2002 edition with information based on Friday's closing.

The first thing I notice is that there were 362 new 52-week highs on the list. It's too many to work with. We need a way to limit the number of stocks we research to keep the process manageable. The reason I decided to use the *IBD* 52-week highs list is that it gives us not only the names of stocks making new highs but also their industry classification and some information on earnings trends. So right away, we can begin to narrow our list of candidates directly by *excluding defensive issues*.

DEFENSIVE FILTER

The list of new 52-week high prices is composed of the industries shown in Table 9-1.

TABLE 9-1: DISTRIBUTION OF INDUSTRIES IN THE NEW 52-WEEK HIGHS LIST

Industry Group	Stocks Making New 52-Week Highs	Industry Group	Stocks Making New 52-Week Highs
Banks	65	Auto and parts	6
Medical	37	Apparel	6
Miscellaneous	25	Telecom	5
Savings and Loans	24	Internet	5
Retail	23	Chemicals	5
Food / Beverage	20	Alcohol/Tobacco	5
Finance	16	Transport	4
Business Service	13	Steel	4
Energy	12	Business Products	4
Leisure	11	Agriculture	3
Computers	11	Office	2
Building	11	Mining	2
Insurance	9	Machinery	2
Electronics	8	Aircraft	2
Utility	7	Real Estate	1
Print/Publishing	7		
Consumer	7	**Total**	**362**

Referring back to the list in Chapter 8, we eliminate the following defensive industries because historically they do not spawn winners:

Banks (65)

Miscellaneous (25)

Savings and Loan (24)

Utility (7)

Mining (these are gold stocks, which are on our defensive list) (2)

Real Estate (1)

So we've reduced our list down by 124 issues. The new number, 238, is more manageable, but it's still far too many stocks to gather data on. To further reduce the list of candidates, let's look at the Earnings Per Share percentile rank published next to each stock name on the *IBD* list. It's a percentile ranking system, 99 the highest, one the lowest, of earnings growth. Obviously, we want growing companies (and we'll use our growth factor to validate the sustainability of the earnings growth trend in a later step). For now, I'll arbitrarily use a minimum EPS ranking of 80 as the screening device. Any stocks that don't have an earnings growth rate better than 80 percent of the stocks in the market will be thrown out. (Later, we'll use an online, free, computer-based stock screening system as a beginning point, so we won't need to use EPS ranking at all. If you were working with a much-smaller list of new-highs, you could also skip it.)

After applying the minimum 80 EPS ranking, the ranks are thinned dramatically to the list of 92 ticker symbols shown in Table 9-2.

TABLE 9-2: PROSPECT LIST AFTER APPLYING THE EPS FILTER

Industry Group	Ticker Symbol	Industry Group	Ticker Symbol	Industry Group	Ticker Symbol
AIRCRAFT	CVU	FOOD/BEVERAGE	LNY	MEDICAL	OLGC
ALCOHOL/TOBACCO	STZ	FOOD/BEVERAGE	PBG	MEDICAL	RCI
APPAREL	GAN	FOOD/BEVERAGE	PEP	MEDICAL	STJ
AUTO&PARTS	AAP	FOOD/BEVERAGE	PZZA	MEDICAL	TGH
BUILDING	AAON	FOOD/BEVERAGE	RI	MEDICAL	THC
BUILDING	GLYT	FOOD/BEVERAGE	TENT	MEDICAL	TRI
BUILDING	MTH	INSURANCE	CTGI	MEDICAL	UNH
BUILDING	NTK	LEISURE	AGY	MEDICAL	VAR
BUILDING	THO	LEISURE	ASCA	MEDICAL	WLP
BUILDING	WLS	LEISURE	BYD	PRINT/PUB	CRRC
BUILDING	WMSI	LEISURE	DFXI	PRINT/PUB	TLX
BUS PRODS	BEL	LEISURE	EPAX	RETAIL	CACOA
BUS PRODS	TONS	LEISURE	FHR	RETAIL	CHBS
BUS SERVICES	BDMS	LEISURE	PENN	RETAIL	COH
BUS SERVICES	PDX	LEISURE	SHFL	RETAIL	CRMT
BUS SERVICES	USLB	MEDICAL	ABC	RETAIL	FCFS
COMPUTERS	INFM	MEDICAL	ACDO	RETAIL	FSM
COMPUTERS	MEDW	MEDICAL	ATH	RETAIL	HHS
COMPUTERS	SSNC	MEDICAL	DCAI	RETAIL	JOSB
CONSUMER	DIIBF	MEDICAL	DGX	RETAIL	KSS
CONSUMER	DLI	MEDICAL	ESRX	RETAIL	LIN
CONSUMER	HB	MEDICAL	GTIV	RETAIL	ROST
CONSUMER	NBTY	MEDICAL	HCA	RETAIL	SCSS
ELECTRONICS	ELSE	MEDICAL	HMA	RETAIL	SCVL
ENERGY	E	MEDICAL	HSIC	RETAIL	URBN
ENERGY	PHEL	MEDICAL	HTRN	RETAIL	WSM
FINANCE	CACC	MEDICAL	LH	STEEL	MRY
FINANCE	JNC	MEDICAL	MME	TELECOM	ROS
FINANCE	MAXF	MEDICAL	NBSC	TELECOM	SHEN
FOOD/BEVERAGE	DOL	MEDICAL	ODSY	TRANSPORT	CLDN
FOOD/BEVERAGE	KOF	MEDICAL	OHP		

In my opinion the list is now a manageable size and we can move on to the next step in the selection process, which is to calculate the growth factor.

RANK CANDIDATES BY GROWTH FACTOR

For this step we need to do some data-gathering and number-crunching. As you will recall, the stock price trends tell us if the company's prospects are improving but we need to verify that the value proposition of the company to its customers is sound—that there is something driving the stock's increase other than one-time expense reductions, optimistic expectations, or hype. The most trustworthy reported number that we can use to determine this is the engine of earnings, sales growth. So we want to give highest priority to the stocks of companies that have not only the best market share-price performance but also the best underlying demand for their products. That is how we came up with the growth factor:

$$\text{Growth Factor} = (\text{One-Year Share Price Growth Percent}) \times (\text{One-Year Sales Growth Percent})$$

Before we can calculate this index for each company, we obviously need to gather raw input data. Since we're concentrating on free public sources of information for this example, I used the following Internet resources:

- One-Year Sales Growth Percent: *Yahoo! Finance* (Company Profile), and *Quicken.com.*

- One-Year Share Price Growth: *Yahoo! Finance* (Company Profile)

Obviously, many other sources on the Web have this kind of data. Whenever you're gathering data and will be investing based on that data, it's always a good idea to cross-check what you find out in two or more sources. The sources don't have to agree completely, but if they are far apart, keep asking questions until you find out why they're different. Having said that, I do consider the two sources listed to be fairly reliable.

Using a spreadsheet program for assembling the data, we calculate growth factors and rank our 92 stocks. Using the *Yahoo* and *Quicken* sources and Microsoft Excel, I was able to rank our 92 ticker symbols on growth factors within about an hour. Naturally, in Table 9-3 the candidates are ranked in descending order with the most attractive companies at the top of the list.

TABLE 9-3: CANDIDATES RANKED BY GROWTH FACTOR

Industry	Symbol	1-Year Sales Growth (percent)	1-Year Share Price Growth (percent)	Growth Factor[1]
MEDICAL	DCAI	114	852	97128
BUSINESS PRODUCTS	BEL	187	182	34034
LEISURE	ASCA	88	327	28776
LEISURE	PENN	77	235	18001
FOOD/BEVERAGE	TENT	27	352	9504
INSURANCE	CTGI	75	124	9300
LEISURE	DFXI	82	107	8774
BUILDING	MTH	43	160	6880
MEDICAL	ODSY	53	118	6207
FOOD/BEVERAGE	LNY	43	141	6063
MEDICAL	TRI	116	46	5336
COMPUTERS	MEDW	16	316	5056
BUS SERVICES	PDX	46	92	4223
FINANCE	MAXF	17	205	3485
TELECOM	SHEN	49	67	3256
MEDICAL	NBSC	21	154	3234
CONSUMER	NBTY	29	107	3103
RETAIL	URBN	18	166	3021
RETAIL	COH	19	135	2579
MEDICAL	ACDO	29	82	2337
BUILDING	WMSI	15	144	2160
MEDICAL	WLP	35	61	2129
FINANCE	CACC	19	107	2033
STEEL	MRY	14	136	1904
BUILDING	WLS	12	140	1708
MEDICAL	MME	23	74	1695
RETAIL	CHBS	32	53	1691
BUILDING	THO	8	182	1474
CONSUMER	DLI	13	115	1472
RETAIL	WSM	15	100	1460
BUS SERVICES	USLB	48	30	1440
ALCOHOL/TOBACCO	STZ	18	77	1386
MEDICAL	ESRX	36	38	1368
RETAIL	SCVL	14	97	1358
MEDICAL	ATH	19	68	1292
APPAREL	GAN	8	140	1176
MEDICAL	THC	14	74	1029
MEDICAL	ABC	39	26	1014
MEDICAL	HMA	18	53	965
ENERGY	PHEL	19	50	950
RETAIL	ROST	11	83	930
RETAIL	FSM	6	143	787
MEDICAL	TGH	14	55	765
LEISURE	AGY	13	55	710
MEDICAL	RCI	21	33	703

TABLE 9-3: CANDIDATES RANKED BY GROWTH FACTOR, *CONT'D*

Industry	Symbol	1-Year Sales Growth (percent)	1-Year Share Price Growth (percent)	Growth Factor
MEDICAL	STJ	15	46	695
MEDICAL	LH	15	47	686
RETAIL	LIN	17	39	663
TELECOM	ROS	6	106	636
MEDICAL	HTRN	30	21	630
LEISURE	SHFL	17	36	616
MEDICAL	OHP	8	78	585
CONSUMER	DIIBF	21	27	567
RETAIL	KSS	22	26	564
MEDICAL	DGX	7	73	518
FINANCE	JNC	8	64	512
RETAIL	JOSB	2	192	442
MEDICAL	VAR	11	40	436
MEDICAL	UNH	10	42	416
RETAIL	FCFS	4	84	336
PRINT/PUB	TLX	5	62	310
RETAIL	CACOA	6	51	291
FOOD/BEVERAGE	PBG	6	48	288
LEISURE	EPAX	8	33	264
FOOD/BEVERAGE	KOF	4	59	236
FOOD/BEVERAGE	RI	5	47	235
MEDICAL	HCA	8	26	200
AUTO&PARTS	AAP	10	20	200
MEDICAL	HSIC	7	26	192
BUILDING	AAON	2	126	189
FOOD/BEVERAGE	PEP	6	28	168
LEISURE	FHR	2	82	164
PRINT/PUB	CRRC	1	80	112
FOOD/BEVERAGE	PZZA	3	15	45
CONSUMER	HB	1	40	32
ENERGY	E	2	13	26
FOOD/BEVERAGE	DOL	-1	110	-110
BUILDING	GLYT	-4	48	-168
RETAIL	HHS	-5	48	-216
BUS SERVICES	BDMS	-1	365	-365
MEDICAL	GTIV	-9	44	-378
BUILDING	NTK	-10	55	-534
TRANSPORT	CLDN	-5	113	-565
LEISURE	BYD	-3	296	-888
BUS PRODS	TONS	-13	76	-988
COMPUTERS	SSNC	-7	158	-1106
ELECTRONICS	ELSE	-23	54	-1242
RETAIL	SCSS	-3	420	-1260
MEDICAL	OLGC	-34	50	-1700
AIRCRAFT	CVU	-48	54	-2592
COMPUTERS	INFM	-26	270	-7020
RETAIL	CRMT	-31	297	-9207

[1]Growth Factor = One-Year Share Price x One-Year Sales Growth Percent.

We now have an objective basis, the growth factor, for ranking portfolio candidates from most to least attractive.

At this point, number crunching gets much easier. Since we're looking for 10 final selections for our portfolio, to save time from now on we'll just gather data on the top 30 stocks in Table 9-3. I'm guessing that this will give us enough stocks that at least 10 will pass the rest of our filters.

OVEREXTENDED FILTER

With our new, narrower list of 30 securities, let's start applying our other screening criteria with the overextended filter. This is where we see how far above the 50-day moving average the stocks are currently trading and eliminate any that are trading at more than 25 percent above the moving average. (*Reminder:* All will be above the 50-day because the list includes only stocks making new highs for the year.)

Of course, we first have to assemble on our spreadsheet the closing price and the 50-day moving average price. This time, I'm going to use another free Internet resource, *StockCharts.com*. With *StockCharts.com,* when I punch in a ticker symbol, I get a chart that includes not just the current closing price but the actual value of the 50-day moving average, to two decimal points. Then I set up a column on my spreadsheet to calculate how far the current price is above the 50-day MA as a percent of the moving average. More specifically,

$$\text{Percent above 50-day MA} = \frac{(\text{Closing Price} - \text{50-day MA value})}{(\text{50-day MA value})} \times 100.$$

Table 9-4 shows us the results we obtain by gathering the data and performing the calculation for each security on the list (still listed in descending growth factor order).

As you can see from the boldfaced items in the right-hand column of Table 9-4, 12 issues are more than 25 percent above their 50-day moving average and may be ripe for a swift price correction. *A word to the wise:* Occasionally these overextended stocks keep going even further above their 50-day MA and don't stop until they have doubled or tripled in price within a short time. Never conclude that you should sell a stock you already own simply because it has done well for you and is now far above its 50-day line. Otherwise you may cut yourself out of some meteoric rises. But that doesn't mean these are good prospects to buy, especially when there are other options that are not overextended.

Eliminating these 12 overextended issues leaves us with 17 issues on which to apply our final filters.

TABLE 9-4: OVEREXTENDED CALCULATIONS FOR PROSPECT LIST

Industry	Ticker Symbol	1-Year Sales Growth	1-Year Share Price Growth	Growth Factor	Share Price	50-Day MA	% Above 50-Day MA
MEDICAL	DCAI	114	852	97,128	6.76	3.67	*84.2%*
BUS PRODS	BEL	187	182	34,034	18.47	14.32	*29.0%*
LEISURE	ASCA	88	327	28,776	32.42	27.02	20.0%
LEISURE	PENN	77	235	18,001	40.20	34.94	15.1%
FOOD/BEV	TENT	27	352	9,504	11.75	8.18	*43.6%*
INSURANCE	CTGI	75	124	9,300	3.36	2.24	*50.0%*
LEISURE	DFXI	82	107	8,774	42.79	33.62	*27.3%*
BUILDING	MTH	43	160	6,880	90.05	65.60	*37.3%*
MEDICAL	ODSY	53	118	6,207	34.85	28.30	23.1%
FOOD/BEV	LNY	43	141	6,063	26.50	24.56	7.9%
MEDICAL	TRI	116	46	5,336	39.35	33.21	18.5%
COMPUTERS	MEDW	16	316	5,056	9.19	6.61	*39.0%*
BUS SERVICES	PDX	46	92	4,223	47.84	40.48	18.2%
FINANCE	MAXF	17	205	3,485	7.03	5.72	22.9%
TELECOM	SHEN	49	67	3,256	50.35	38.20	*31.8%*
MEDICAL	NBSC	21	154	3,234	10.40	8.20	*26.8%*
CONSUMER	NBTY	29	107	3,103	19.07	16.15	18.1%
RETAIL	URBN	18	166	3,021	30.30	24.82	22.1%
RETAIL	COH	19	135	2,579	55.42	49.40	12.2%
MEDICAL	ACDO	29	82	2,337	62.78	55.03	14.1%
BUILDING	WMSI	15	144	2,160	8.00	5.46	*46.5%*
MEDICAL	WLP	35	61	2,129	71.54	63.40	12.8%
FINANCE	CACC	19	107	2,033	13.25	10.91	21.4%
STEEL	MRY	14	136	1,904	2.55	1.69	*50.9%*
BUILDING	WLS	12	140	1,708	23.77	21.04	13.0%
MEDICAL	MME	23	74	1,695	33.00	27.85	18.5%
RETAIL	CHBS	32	53	1,691	38.60	31.65	22.0%
BUILDING	THO	8	182	1,474	59.20	49.07	20.6%
CONSUMER	DLI	13	115	1,472	23.10	18.36	*25.8%*

THINLY TRADED FILTER AND EXCESSIVE VALUATION ASSESSMENT

Adding a column or two to the spreadsheet we're building, we put in the average daily trading volume (the number of days used to calculate average daily trading volume is not critical, but the longer the period used, the better the reading is likely to be on the true long-term liquidity for each stock), and the price to sales ratio. Both of these items are readily available from *Yahoo! Finance* as part of its Detailed Quotes format.

After we eliminated the overextended stocks we are left with the 17 stocks shown in Table 9-5, still in descending order by growth factor but now with average daily trading volume and price-to-sales ratio added. We want to eliminate the items that have trading volumes less than 50,000 shares per day. The Average Daily Column has two issues that do not make the cut and should be highlighted for removal from the prospect list.

TABLE 9-5: THINLY TRADED AND PRICE-TO-SALES RATIO FILTERS APPLIED TO PROPECT LIST

Industry	Ticker Symbol	1-Year Sales Growth	1-Year Share Price Growth	Growth Factor	Share Price	50-Day MA	% Above 50-Day MA	Average Daily Volume (1,000s)*	P/S Ratio*
LEISURE	ASCA	88	327	28,776	32.42	27.02	20.0%	187	1.3
LEISURE	PENN	77	235	18,001	40.20	34.94	15.1%	383	1.5
MEDICAL	ODSY	53	118	6,207	34.85	28.30	23.1%	159	4.1
FOOD/BEV	LNY	43	141	6,063	26.50	24.56	7.9%	197	0.8
MEDICAL	TRI	116	46	5,336	39.35	33.21	18.5%	442	1.1
BUS SERV	PDX	46	92	4,223	47.84	40.48	18.2%	167	3.4
FINANCE	MAXF	17	205	3,485	7.03	5.72	22.9%	51	0.4
CONSUMER	NBTY	29	107	3,103	19.07	16.15	18.1%	649	1.5
RETAIL	URBN	18	166	3,021	30.30	24.82	22.1%	192	1.5
RETAIL	COH	19	135	2,579	55.42	49.40	12.2%	357	3.7
MEDICAL	ACDO	29	82	2,337	62.78	55.03	14.1%	672	3.1
MEDICAL	WLP	35	61	2,129	71.54	63.40	12.8%	828	0.8
FINANCE	CACC	19	107	2,033	13.25	10.91	21.4%	*31*	3.8
BUILDING	WLS	12	140	1708	23.77	21.04	13.0%	54	0.5
MEDICAL	MME	23	74	1695	33.00	27.85	18.5%	334	0.9
RETAIL	CHBS	32	53	1691	38.60	31.65	22.0%	513	3.5
BUILDING	THO	8	182	1474	59.20	49.07	20.6%	*38*	0.9
RETAIL	WSM	15	100	1460	55.69	46.75	19.1%	600	1.5

Source: Yahoo! Finance

APPLIED TO PROSPECT LIST

This would probably be a good time to review the remaining 15 stocks just to make sure that nothing still on the list is at the far extremes of market valuation relative to sales. This appears in the right-hand column in Table 9-6.

There is only one security over 4.0 on the P/S ratio and just four more are over 3.0. In other words, the range of valuations is reasonable, with the whole group averaging out at 1.9. While this isn't cheap, remember we're not looking for cheap stocks; we're looking for good stocks. You have to pay up some for stocks that have a high chance of making good-sized moves. Cheap stocks, like cheap suits, are no good. At any rate, there doesn't seem to be inordinate amounts of optimism built into most of the stocks on the prospect list.

TABLE 9-6: PRICE-TO-SALES RATIO APPLIED TO REMAINING PROSPECTS

Industry	Ticker Symbol	1-Year Sales Growth	1-Year Share Price Growth	Growth Factor	Share Price	50-Day MA	% Above 50-Day MA	Average Daily Volume (1,000s)	P/S Ratio
LEISURE	ASCA	88	327	28,776	32.42	27.02	20.0%	187	1.3
LEISURE	PENN	77	235	18,001	40.20	34.94	15.1%	383	1.5
MEDICAL	ODSY	53	118	6,207	34.85	28.30	23.1%	159	4.1
FOOD/BEV	LNY	43	141	6,063	26.50	24.56	7.9%	197	0.8
MEDICAL	TRI	116	46	5,336	39.35	33.21	18.5%	442	1.1
BUS SERV	PDX	46	92	4,223	47.84	40.48	18.2%	167	3.4
FINANCE	MAXF	17	205	3,485	7.03	5.72	22.9%	51	0.4
CONSUMER	NBTY	29	107	3,103	19.07	16.15	18.1%	649	1.5
RETAIL	URBN	18	166	3,021	30.30	24.82	22.1%	192	1.5
RETAIL	COH	19	135	2,579	55.42	49.40	12.2%	357	3.7
MEDICAL	ACDO	29	82	2,337	62.78	55.03	14.1%	672	3.1
MEDICAL	WLP	35	61	2,129	71.54	63.40	12.8%	828	0.8
BUILDING	WLS	12	140	1,708	23.77	21.04	13.0%	54	0.5
MEDICAL	MME	23	74	1,695	33.00	27.85	18.5%	334	0.9
RETAIL	CHBS	32	53	1,691	38.60	31.65	22.0%	513	3.5
RETAIL	WSM	15	100	1,460	55.69	46.75	19.1%	600	1.5

INDUSTRY CONCENTRATION REVIEW

So now it's time to choose the 10 stocks we'll actually buy. Naturally we want the 10 with the highest growth factor ranking under normal circumstances. Let's see if the top 10 stocks represent a reasonable level of industry diversification (Table 9-7).

The largest industry groups represented here are Medical, Leisure, and Retail, each of which is 20 percent of the portfolio (two of 10 issues). Food/Beverage, Business Services, Finance, and Consumer are all at 10

TABLE 9-7: TOP 10 STOCKS

Industry	Ticker Symbol	1-Year Sales Growth	1-Year Share Price Growth	Growth Factor	Share Price	50-Day MA	% Above 50-Day MA	Average Daily Volume (1,000s)	P/S Ratio
LEISURE	ASCA	88	327	28,776	32.42	27.02	20.0%	187	1.3
LEISURE	PENN	77	235	18,001	40.20	34.94	15.1%	383	1.5
MEDICAL	ODSY	53	118	6,207	34.85	28.30	23.1%	159	4.1
FOOD/BEV	LNY	43	141	6,063	26.50	24.56	7.9%	197	0.8
MEDICAL	TRI	116	46	5,336	39.35	33.21	18.5%	442	1.1
BUS SERV	PDX	46	92	4,223	47.84	40.48	18.2%	167	3.4
FINANCE	MAXF	17	205	3,485	7.03	5.72	22.9%	51	0.4
CONSUMER	NBTY	29	107	3,103	19.07	16.15	18.1%	649	1.5
RETAIL	URBN	18	166	3,021	30.30	24.82	22.1%	192	1.5
RETAIL	COH	19	135	2,579	55.42	49.40	12.2%	357	3.7

percent, which brings the total to 100 percent. Seven industries represented is not bad for a 10-stock portfolio, but we might have some concern about the concentration in medical stocks because if we dig a little deeper into the business models of PDX and NBTY, we find that, though they were classified by *IBD* as being in non-medical industries, their businesses are both closely related to medical: PDX is providing physician-management services, and NBTY is a provider of nutritional supplements. In other words, once we look behind the classifications, we find that about 40 percent of our portfolio selections are actually in medical-related stocks. That is about as much as you'd want to see in a single industry, in my opinion, even in an aggressive growth portfolio. If you wanted a more conservative industry allocation, you could go further down the list to prospects discarded earlier and substitute something else for your lowest-ranking medical stocks—NBTY, TRI, ODSY, in that order, working up from the lowest growth factor because we want to maximize the growth factor of our entire portfolio as much as possible while still maintaining diversification. For the purposes of our example, however, we'll tolerate the borderline situation in medical stocks and use the 10 stocks listed as our final selection.

Let's re-check the P/S ratio once again just for these 10 selections: With an average P/S ratio of 1.9, we're well within the reasonable range of optimistically-valued stocks. Again, they're not cheap, but they're not all in the upper 10 percent of market valuations relative to sales, either.

CAPITALIZATION REVIEW

We now need to review our selections quickly to make sure we don't have a portfolio of extremely large-cap stocks, the type that, like glaciers, won't move very far or very fast. Although we can see at a glance that there aren't too many celebrity stocks here, let's visit *Yahoo! Finance* again, and capture the market capitalization of each selection (see Table 9-8).

These days, anything less than $1 billion in market value is considered small-cap. Looks like we've got mostly small-caps and near-small-caps here—not surprising, because small-caps are doing well right now in terms of both market and business performance. Because we let the market and business performance pick our stocks, we've found the performers. No need to weed out giant, large-cap stocks.

TABLE 9-8: MARKET CAPITALIZATION OF TOP 10 STOCKS

Ticker Symbol	Total Market Capitalization, $ Billions
ASCA	0.9
PENN	0.8
ODSY	0.5
LNY	0.6
TRI	2.7
PDX	1.2
MAXF	.05
NBTY	1.1
URBN	0.5
COH	2.3

To keep things in perspective: Of the 30 Dow Jones Industrial Average stocks, the largest are GE and Microsoft at over $300 billion each, the smallest are Eastman Kodak at $9 billion and Caterpillar at $18 billion. Most Dow components are in the $30 billion to $80 billion range. I draw my personal line at a maximum of $100 billion in capitalization for a company in an aggressive portfolio, and I wouldn't want more than one. Anything bigger is just too large to grow really quickly. (Obviously, the cutoff number is an ever-changing target as market caps of all stocks ebb and grow, and it's not objective, it's an arbitrary number picked by personal preference.)

It's also true that once in a while large-cap stocks are the real market stars. If your analysis using the method I've described leads you to large-caps, buy them. But even in times of favor for large-caps, the extremely large-cap stocks (right now, $100 billion and up) usually don't perform as well as even the slightly smaller ones.

We would also want to review the portfolio to make sure that low-priced shares don't dominate it. There's only one of our selections trading below $15 per share (MAXF), so we're OK in the share-price department. As a general rule of thumb, it's probably wiser not to have more than 20 percent of a portfolio devoted to stocks selling below $15 per share.

CHART SCAN (POST-BUYOUT FILTER AND VOLATILITY FILTER)

We now have our 10 selections. Let's do a chart review, on the outside chance that one of these selections will show either excessive volatility (i.e., a history of not trending well) or is on the verge of being acquired by another firm. To do this, let's look at a short-term chart for each issue (Figures 9-1 through 9-10, pages 109-113). On these charts, each bar represents one week of trading. The charts cover about five quarters, except the one for ODSY (Figure 9-3), a relatively new issue with less than a year's trading history.

Looking over the one-year charts for our 10 selections, none of them show a discontinuous gap in trading that would indicate that it's in the process of being acquired by another firm. That's good.

Except for one stock (TRI), none seem to be overly erratic or choppy. All have made good moves over the past year and have fairly tight trading ranges compared to the percentage moves they have made. The one possible exception is Triad Hospitals (TRI). Although Triad is making a new price high for the year, it doesn't seem to have made much headway during the past year. For this stock, we'd better look at a longer-term chart to see if the stock has any history at all of trending well. I'd like to look at a five-year chart, but since I only have about two-and-a-half years of data (TRI went public in 1999), that's what we'll look at (Figure 9-11, page 114).

The long-term chart for Triad shows that despite its short history, the stock is definitely capable of sustaining a sizeable trend. It appears to be moving out of a one-year-plus price consolidation, a good sign. So we'll keep all 10 of our selections in our portfolio.

CHARTING RESOURCES

To implement what you learn in this book, you will need access to data and some tools to analyze it. As we have seen, any numerical data you need for selection and analysis is available free online. You can use online charts for chart analysis, too.

Great charting resources are:

- *StockCharts.com* and *BigCharts.com*. These will all construct charts to your parameters, including candlestick charts.

FIGURES 9-1: AMERISTAR CASINOS (ASCA)

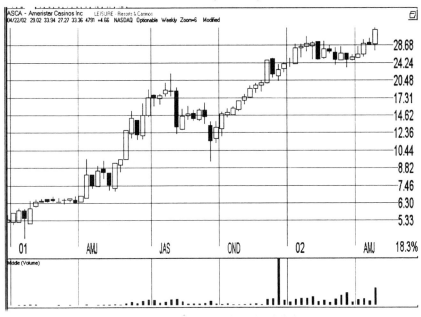

FIGURE 9-2: PENN NATIONAL GAMING INC (PENN)

FIGURES 9-3: ODYSSEY HEALTHCARE INC (ODSY)

FIGURE 9-4: LANDRYS RESTAURANTS INC (LNY)

FIGURES 9-5: TRIAD HOSPITALS INC (TRI)

FIGURE 9-6: PEDIATRIX MEDICAL GR INC (PDX)

FIGURES 9-7: MAXCOR FINANCIAL GRP INC (MAXF)

FIGURE 9-8: NBTY INC (NBTY)

FIGURES 9-9: URBAN OUTFITTERS INC (URBN)

FIGURE 9-10: COACH INC (COH)

Nevertheless, personally, I prefer to pay for high-quality charting software, because I like being able to change the perspective and customize charts. So far I've found the TeleChart 2000 program offered by Worden Brothers to offer the best value. For a small monthly subscription fee (currently about $30), you receive several years of data on most of the stocks on the NYSE, AMEX, and NASDAQ, along with daily data updates and a customizable set of tools for zeroing in on stocks that meet your criteria. This makes it easy for you to look at long-term or short-term charts. This program has the advantage of integrating some scanning capabilities. The free Internet resources are slow, so TC2000 has a large advantage in terms of speed as well as ease of use, since the data resides on your PC.

FIGURE 9-11: TRIAD HOSPITALS (TRI)

CHECK THE NEWS

Finally, we want to check the news headlines on all these stocks. Continuing the emphasis on free public information, a simple quote entry into *Yahoo!*'s website gives us all the news headlines on each issue. Scanning these headlines, I'm relieved but not surprised to see no mention of any other firms acquiring any of these firms. A few of the firms are acquiring other firms, but that's an entirely different matter and not a cause for concern. If our firms are acquiring other firms, that's actually a good sign as to their health. They're on the upswing, confirming our selection.

A LESS MANUAL EXAMPLE

The example we've just walked through is highly manual and time-consuming, taking probably one to two hours to construct. There are certainly less manual approaches that can be used, even if we want to continue using only free data tools available on the Internet. For instance, a few days after our manual example, I composed Table 9-9 of high-potential candidates in far less time using MSN's free Custom Stock Screener.

Using MSN's screener, in one single step I was able to narrow down the entire universe of stocks to 24 that had closed above the previous 52-week high, a daily trading volume of at least 50,000 shares, had a high sales growth rate, and had a share price of at least $5. While the screener returned some stocks with a low sales growth rate (it appeared to prioritize share price growth above sales growth, which is appropriate, in my opinion), the results were quite good. By gathering some additional data from *Yahoo! Finance* and applying our other criteria (weeding out defensive industries, screening out items more than 25 percent above the 50-day MA, etc.). I found five solid candidates for purchase: NFI, ASCA, FCN, RGX, and DNCR. None of the five violated our other criteria by having a history of non-trending trading patterns, being extremely large-cap, or the subject of a buyout, having absurdly high P/S ratios, and so on. Neither does there appear to be an unacceptable concentration in any one industry (medical represents two of the five).

This approach took me about half an hour to accomplish from start to finish. Although it only returned five acceptable candidates, there is no reason that we have to find all our candidates for purchase on a single day. In fact, later we'll review reasons why you should spread your purchases out over a number of weeks or months, especially when you're just starting out. We could easily repeat the same exercise the very next day, the next week, or the next month.

There are many, many good, free stock screening utilities on the web besides this one. No doubt you already know of others. If not, simply type

TABLE 9-9: RESULTS OF SEARCH USING MSN CUSTOM STOCK SCREENER AND OTHER SOURCES[4] (APRIL 24, 2002)

Industry	Ticker Symbol	1-Year Revenue Growth (percent)	1-Year Stock Price Growth (percent)	Growth Factor	Closing Price	1-Mo. Average Daily Trading Volume	50-Day Moving Average	Percent Above 50-Day Moving Average	Accepted/Rejected
FINANCE	NFI	142	189	26,838	22.8	63	19.03	20%	**Accepted.**
ENTERTAINMENT	ASCA	83	265	21,995	32.9	203	27.44	20%	**Accepted.**
AUTO SALES	CRMT	45	296	13,320	14.85	67	9.71	**53%**	Too high above 50-day MA.
GOLD MINING	HGMCY	35	185	6,475	13.8	1348	10.66	**29%**	Defensive industry. Too high above 50-day MA.
ELECTRON-ICS	SYPR	18	348	6,264	21.35	211	15.82	**35%**	Too high above 50-day MA.
CONSULT-ING	FCN	23	218	5,014	33.95	135	29.35	16%	**Accepted.**
MEDICAL	HGR	4	1150	4,600	13.75	105	10.34	**33%**	Too high above 50-day MA.
MEDICAL	RGX	12	288	3,456	12.56	102	11.57	9%	Single-digit sales growth.
MEDICAL	DNCR	14	207	2,898	19.4	95	15.94	22%	Single-digit sales growth.
RETAIL	SGDE	10	277	2,770	7.32	119	5.19	**41%**	Single-digit sales growth. Too high above 50-day MA.
MEDICAL	MTEC	6	293	1,758	41.27	243	30.82	**34%**	Single-digit sales growth. Too high above 50-day MA.
APPAREL	MWRK	6	265	1,590	28.79	76	17.07	**69%**	Single-digit sales growth. Too high above 50-day MA.
AUTO SALES	SAH	5	248	1,240	35.5	298	29.77	19%	Single-digit sales growth.
DIVERSIFIED	GFF	4	153	612	19.95	189	18.05	11%	Single-digit sales growth.
PACKAGING	SLGN	3	195	585	40.49	88	33.42	21%	Single-digit sales growth.
FINANCE	MAXF	2	175	350	7.42	74	5.79	**28%**	Single-digit sales growth. Too high above 50-day MA.
REC. VEHICLES	THO	-8	177	-1416	61.24	54	50.12	22%	Negative sales growth.
MEDICAL	SIE	-7	209	-1463	15.9	173	12.34	**29%**	Negative sales growth. Too high above 50-day MA.
GOLD MINING	*GOLD*	*-10*	165	-1650	11.83	2464	9.28	**27%**	Negative sales growth.
RETAIL	SKO	*-10*	175	-1750	22.26	311	17.09	**30%**	Too high above 50-day MA.
JEWELRY	CTHR	*-10*	353	-3530	5.75	66	4	**44%**	Negative sales growth.
CONSUMER	CHTT	*-22*	212	-4664	31.16	190	21.62	**44%**	Negative sales growth.
ENTERTAINMENT	MVL	*-22*	357	-7854	9.1	368	7.22	**26%**	Negative sales growth.
RESTAURANTS	CKR	*-19*	435	-8265	12.75	438	10.13	**26%**	Too high above 50-day MA.

TABLE 9-9: RESULTS OF SEARCH, APRIL 24, 2002 USING MSN CUSTOM STOCK SCREENER AND OTHER SOURCES, CONT'D

Industry	Ticker Symbol	1-Year Revenue Growth (percent)	1-Year Stock Price Growth (percent)	Growth Factor	Closing Price	1-Mo Average Daily Trading Volume	50-Day Moving Average	Percent Above 50-Day Moving Average	Accepted/Rejected
REC. VEHICLES	THO	-8	177	-1416	61.24	54	50.12	22%	Negative sales growth.
MEDICAL	SIE	-7	209	-1463	15.9	175	12.34	29%	Negative sales growth.
GOLD MINING	GOLD	*-10*	165	*-1650*	11.83	2464	9.28	*27%*	Too high above 50-day MA.
RETAIL	SKO	*-10*	175	*-1750*	22.26	311	17.09	*30%*	Too high above 50-day MA.
JEWELRY	CTHR	*-10*	353	*-3530*	5.75	66	4	*44%*	Negative sales growth. Too high above 50-day MA.
CONSUMER	CHTT	*-22*	212	*-4664*	31.16	150	21.62	*44%*	Negative sales growth. Too high above 50-day MA.
ENTERTAINMENT	MVL	*-22*	357	*-7854*	9.1	368	7.22	*26%*	Negative sales growth. Too high above 50-day MA.
RESTAURANTS	CKR	*-19*	435	*-8265*	12.75	438	10.13	*26%*	Negative sales growth. Too high above 50-day MA.

Note: Unacceptable results are boldfaced and italicized.

[a]Industry information using *Yahoo! Finance* Company Profiles.

Screening results using MSN's Custom Stock Screener (*http://moneycentral.msn.com/investor/finder*)
Previous Day's Closing Price, >=52-week high
Rev Growth Year vs. Year, High as Possible
Percent Price Change Last Year, High as Possible
Average Daily Volume Last Month, >=50,000
Share Price >=$5

MSN Customer Stock Screener was also the data source for One-Year Revenue Growth (Percent), One-Year Stock Price Growth (Percent), Closing Price, and One-Month Average Daily Trading Volume.

50-Day Moving Average data was obtained from *StockCharts.com* "stock screener" into your favorite search engine; you'll probably find one you enjoy using. Don't expect any of them to have perfect data; double-check sources before you actually buy anything, just to be certain they're accurate. For instance, in both our previous manual example and this one, we were led to consider MAXF as one of the possibilities, but there's quite a large difference between the one-year revenue growth number used by the MSN screener and the one used by *Yahoo! Finance.*

Different reporting periods and cutoffs and the like may cause these differences. Still, the difference actually changed our attitude to MAXF, which we found acceptable in the previous exercise but not in this one. The moral of the story is that different data and reporting periods may skew results, so check out the specifics on your final candidates list several different ways before you buy.

ACTUAL PRICES VERSUS PLANNED PRICES

Now that we've selected our portfolio, how do we get into these stocks, and at what price? The best policy here is to keep it simple. Buy at the next available price. In our portfolio example, we can't get into these stocks at the price they closed at yesterday; we must wait until the market opens. The opening prices on the Monday after the weekend they were selected are shown in Table 9-10.

TABLE 9-10: OPENING PRICES FOR TOP 10 STOCKS

Ticker Symbol	Closing Price on Friday, April 19, 2002	Opening Price on Monday, April 22, 2002
ASCA	32.42	33.46
PENN	40.20	40.21
ODSY	34.85	35.84
LNY	26.50	26.55
TRI	39.35	39.20
PDX	47.84	47.84
MAXF	7.03	7.20
NBTY	19.07	19.20
URBN	30.30	30.23
COH	55.42	55.67

When you are going to buy stocks, always use a *market order*. Don't succumb to the emotionally alluring, but foolish practice of placing limit orders. If you do, eventually the best of the stocks you've selected get away from you, never coming back to where you set your limit order. Unfortunately, the stocks that may be entering a temporary (or permanent) downtrend do dutifully come back to fill your limit order. You'll be stuck with the losers, and you'll never buy the winners you selected.

Doesn't sound too appealing, does it? Yet it's amazing the number of experienced investors who place limit orders throughout their entire lifetimes and never figure out why their results aren't very good. If your experience has been that your limit orders *are* usually filled when placed below the market, it probably means you haven't been buying the right kinds of stocks. High-potential stocks spend more time moving forward than they do retreating.

I recently placed a market order for a stock and had it filled on a "gap" opening about 5 percent higher than the previous close. At the end of the day it closed almost 50 percent above the opening price. Had I used a limit order, I would never have got it. Of course, things don't always work out so nicely, but in the long run you hurt yourself more than you help yourself by using limit orders.

However, if you place your orders before the market opens and want to protect yourself from an outrageous breakaway gap opening, then place a limit order that is 3 percent to 5 percent *above* (not below) the previous closing price. You'll most likely still get filled at the opening price, but won't stack the odds too far against you in the long run, as people do when they place limit orders below the market. By far, the best policy is to use market orders, though.

For the purposes of our sample portfolio and future examples based on it, we'll assume the orders for our 10 stocks were filled at Monday's opening price (see Table 9-10).

CHAPTER SUMMARY

Once you know the correct criteria to use, finding high-potential stocks is not hard, but it does take some work. This process can be done manually as we've just done or using any number of free online stock screening utilities. Either way you opt to do your prospecting, make sure you go through all the steps and apply *all* the criteria.

SECTION III
PORTFOLIO MANAGEMENT

CHAPTER 10 —————
PORTFOLIO MANAGEMENT
TECHNIQUES

Obviously, it's not enough to only know how to select stocks—unless you're omniscient and can predict with total accuracy, which stocks were going to go up, and by how much. Since none of us are, we need a sound system for telling us when to give up on a stock we've bought and cut our losses. We also need to know when, if ever, to add to an existing position, how much of each stock to buy in the first place, etc. Most books on the stock market don't say much about things like these. They may purport to tell you when to sell by supplying a laundry list of highly subjective rules, but there seems to be no integrated framework for viewing and managing the portfolio as a whole.

In this section we explore both good and bad portfolio management policy in order to point out the differences clearly. Then, we'll use the principles learned to create a realistic, sound means of managing a portfolio for maximum gains and minimum losses.

THE WORLD'S WORST PORTFOLIO SYSTEM AND WHAT IT TEACHES US

Before we take the next step down our road to investment success, let's digress a bit and review the worst stock-trading approach for stocks that can be imagined. This is a simple system known as scale trading. Why would we want to learn about the worst system? Because once we know the worst possible system, one that is destined to maximize losses over the long run, then we can reverse engineer it to craft a portfolio management system that does just the opposite—one that produces some tremendous long-term gains. That's how I came up with the Reverse Scale

System, introduced later in this book. The Reverse Scale System is a portfolio management philosophy that will serve you well once you understand it, but I want you to know not only what the system is but also to understand how it was developed and why it works. Understanding the worst system—scale trading—is the key to understanding why its reverse is a very good approach.

Note, though, that my negative comments on scale trading apply only when it's used with stocks. Scale trading *can* be a viable system when it's applied to commodities or other tangible items with inherent value, meaning that they cannot decline to zero value except in the very rare case that the commodity becomes obsolete. But even with commodities, scale trading is tricky and requires a lot of capital and advance planning if you're to be successful.[1] Unlike commodities, individual stocks can and do become worthless fairly often, which is a major reason why scale trading is unfit for stock investing. Since all stocks are speculations, we should never assume that any stock is so well founded that it can't decline to zero—or at least go down far enough to effectively wreck your portfolio.

How Scale Trading Works

Other than the fact that it's simple, this system has no redeeming value when it's applied to stocks. It's the manifestation of all the most devastating investor mistakes. While it can produce small profits over short periods, eventually it *always* leads to the poorhouse when applied consistently. Scale trading is not a very popular or widespread system except among extreme neophytes, as anyone using it will not last very long in the stock market. It's the financial equivalent of skydiving without a parachute: It's exciting while the ride lasts, but the good feeling comes to an end very quickly.

Scale trading can be applied to a single stock or a portfolio of stocks with equally disastrous results. This is how it's done: Take an initial position and then add to it in predetermined increments as the position declines in value, and sell any purchases that increase in value. For instance, the investor might buy 20 shares of stock at $50 ($1,000) and decide to buy another $1,000 worth of stock if the price declines by 20

---

[1] For an in-depth look at scale trading as applied by commodities, an excellent resource is Robert F. Wiest's book, *You Can't Lose Trading Commodities.* Westlake Village, CA: Robert F. Wiest, 1992.

percent. If the price increases from $50 before declining to $40, he will sell his 20 shares for $60, making a profit of $200 less commissions. But assume the price doesn't increase. The investor buys another 25 shares at $40 with the idea of selling those acquired at $40 if the price then increases to $50, and so on. The purchase and sale levels for this particular situation are shown in Table 10-1.

TABLE 10-1: AN EXAMPLE OF SCALE TRADING AT 20 PERCENT DECLINING PURCHASE INCREMENTS

Price	Amount Invested This Purchase	Shares Bought This Purchase	Cumulative Dollars Invested	Cumulative Shares Owned	Cumulative Value of Shares	Cumulative Cost/Share	Total Profit/ (Loss)
50	$1,000	20	$1,000	20	$1,000	$50.00	$0
40	$1,000	25	$2,000	45	$1,800	$44.44	($200)
32	$992	31	$2,992	76	$2,432	$39.37	($560)
25 5/8	$998	39	$3,990	115	$2,944	$34.70	($1,046)
20 1/2	$1,004	49	$4,994	164	$3,359	$30.45	($1,635)
16 3/8	$999	61	$5,993	225	$3,686	$26.64	($2,307)
13 1/8	$996	76	$6,989	301	$3,945	$23.22	($3,044)
10 1/2	$996	95	$7,986	396	$4,152	$20.17	($3,833)
8 3/8	$998	119	$8,904	515	$4,320	$17.44	($4,664)
6 3/4	$1,000	149	$9,984	664	$4,456	$13.04	($6,528)
5 3/8	$999	186	$10,982	850	$4,563	$12.92	($6,419)
4 1/4	$1,001	233	$11,983	1083	$4,651	$11.06	($7,332)

The scale trader is hoping to profit by, for example, selling any shares acquired at 32 on a subsequent rise to 40, any shares purchased at 20 1/2 on a rise to 25 5/8, and so on until the stock advances to 60, at which point the scale trader sells off the last of his shares—those bought at 50.

There is no limit to the number of times a stock can oscillate between any two or more of the price levels. Each time this happens the trader pockets another $200 profit, excluding the commissions. He feels great taking these profits—for a while.

It may seem like a foolproof approach to the neophyte trader, but let's trace what happens through a hypothetical situation. Our trader takes his position, buying 20 shares at $50/share. The price then slips to $40, so the investor buys 25 more shares. From there, the price increases to $55, so the 25 shares acquired at 40 were sold at $50, netting a profit before commissions of $200. At this point, the 20 shares acquired at $50 are still in his inventory but he doesn't get to sell those shares, because the price drops from $55 all the way down to $30—by which time he's bought 25 more shares at $40 and another 31 shares at $32—before increasing again to $40. The shares purchased at $32 are sold for $40 for another $200 profit. Fantastic! He has so far generated a $400 realized profit and never had more than $3,000 invested at any point. The only negative so far is that it took four months to do this—but $400 profit on a $3,000 investment over four months is not bad. So far, so good.

From $40, the price then takes another dive down to $15. He buys shares at $32, $25 5/8, $20 1/2, and $16 3/8. Then the price runs up to $30 before retreating back to 25 5/8. Quite a windfall for our trader. He sells the shares acquired at $16 3/8 for $20 1/2, and the ones scooped up at $20 1/2 for $25 5/8. From this, he nets out another $400, bringing his total trading profits to $800. True, he has a $1,046 unrealized loss, which would bring his net profit to a negative $246, but he reasons that when the price goes back up to $60 he will have completed his trade and sold out every single position for a profit. At this time, though, he narrowly misses selling the shares acquired for $25 5/8 at 32, because the price topped out this time at $30.

Next, the unexpected happens. The company that our scale-trading friend is investing in reports that it is under Federal investigation for false financial reporting. The next day, the stock opens a few points lower and just keeps on dropping until it hits $10 3/8, its closing price for the day. Though shaken by the news, our friend is disciplined about his system. He buys slugs of the stock right on schedule at $25 5/8, $20 1/2, $16 3/8, $13 1/8, and $10 1/2. True, he's getting a little worried because he's eight months into this trade and though he has an $800 realized gain he also has a $3,833 unrealized loss. He also is starting to realize that so far he has nothing to show for his nearly $8,000 investment except a net loss. He starts to wake up at night wondering what will happen to his position; although he realized that this could happen, he never thought that it actually *would* happen.

Unfortunately, in the following months the investigation reveals that the company does actually have some fraudulent practices. This means that the balance sheet and income statements for some previous years have to be revised to reflect the effects of the management misstatement and cover-up. The experienced (though crooked) management is ousted for their sins and replaced. The price of the stock works its way lower and eventually levels out between $4 and $5 per share, and it languishes there in the low single digits for the next *five years*.

Our scale-trading friend now has a $6,000 to $7,000 unrealized loss in addition to his $800 trading gain, and 10 or 11 thousand dollars invested in the stock he still holds—even though at the outset, he never really thought he'd have to invest more than a few thousand dollars. Once in a while over the next few years he may get a $200 trading gain as the stock bounces around, but this pales in relation to what he has invested—and what he could have earned even from a passbook savings account. On top of this, he also has to live with the *worry* for the next five years that the stock will further decline, causing him to either give up his system completely or invest even more money. And now he realizes that so much time has passed that even if the stock should ever rise back up to $60, his annual rate of return will be minuscule.

It's scary to realize what can happen when you get caught up in a system as flawed as scale trading. This little story might sound extreme, but I assure you that every single day a few people get the bright idea to do exactly what our poor friend in the story did. Thinking they've discovered a money machine, they begin scale trading and it is simply a matter of time before they're trapped. Worse, many of them have a few months of good experience and they up the ante, deciding to invest several times more per trade than originally envisioned. This merely compounds their losses later on, when the inevitable unforeseen drop occurs.

The trader in the story was disciplined—he held to his system against all the odds—but he still got mired in a terrible mess. The lesson to be learned is that to be successful, you not only have to be disciplined, but you must also base your system or method on a theory that's *correct* as well. *A bad theory, no matter how well implemented, still results in a loss.*

Of course, not every scale trade results in a disaster, as long as the trader realizes the potential before actual disaster strikes. But the potential for profit is always small in relation to the time, worry, and capital invested. The typical pattern with scale trades is a series of small profits followed by one gigantic loss.

Some folks even apply the scale trading technique to several different stocks at the same time. This does nothing but compress the amount of time it takes to find a stock that just keeps declining and declining in value, one that may even become totally worthless and file for bankruptcy. Almost as bad, it may decline from $50 all the way down to $10 per share and sit there, for a long time. It may sit there for years or even decades, trapping the poor trader in his losing position earning little or nothing on his money. Rest assured that anyone who uses this approach consistently in the stock market will fall into this trap fairly early in the process. The fatal assumption made by the scale-trading theory is "what goes down must come up." As I explained earlier, this simply is not the case with stocks.

In the example I gave above, if the price of the stock declines to slightly above $1 per share, the hapless scale trader will own stock with a market value of $4,900 in which he has $17,900 invested—a loss of $13,000. If the company goes bankrupt, the stock would be worthless and the loss would be sickening—at least $17,900, if he had sense enough to stop buying once the stock fell below $1. In this case he started with only $1,000. Usually, the neophyte feels the system is so foolproof that he starts with $5,000 or so.

The only saving grace is that people tend to pursue this system when they're young and foolish and have little money to lose. So if our novice scale trader started with a $10,000 initial position at $50 per share instead of the $1,000 position in the example, he likely won't lose the entire $170,900 we might expect him to lose—because he probably won't have that much.

The positives of scale trading are:

1. It's simple and not subjective.

2. It can generate lots of small gains in choppy market conditions.

The negatives of scale trading are:

1. In a portfolio of stocks, the stocks that do worst absorb the most capital as more and more purchases are made while they decline. Over time, most of the available capital is automatically allocated to the worst-performing stocks while the best stocks are sold off to support them. The result is at best a disastrous underperformance compared to the market or at worst a total loss of capital. A scale trader who uses margin (borrows money from the broker to buy even more stock) may in fact creatively find a way to lose even more money than he has, forcing him into bankruptcy. The biggest problem is that scale trading cuts the trader's gains and lets his losses run—just the opposite of what you as a successful investor would allow.

2. It's impossible to know in advance how much capital it will take to execute the system because you never know how far down a stock will go before it recovers—if it does recover. There are an infinite number of 50 percent declines between any positive number and zero. Therefore, you may have to make an infinite number of purchases to fully execute the system. Few people I know have unlimited capital.

3. Eventually, everyone who practices scale trading buys a stock that declines precipitously and then goes bankrupt. The losses can be huge. There have been a plethora of seemingly rock-solid companies over the years that have ended up in bankruptcy court. Ever heard of Enron?

4. The scale trader never gets the benefit of a favorable trend because he's always selling his winners and buying more of his losers.

5. Even when a scale trade is successful, the amount of profit is very small relative to the amount invested—and especially relative to the risk of catastrophic loss.

6. A scale trader who's locked into a large losing position can't even get the tax benefit of a write-off, because his system makes no provision for selling out losing positions. Of course, if the firm goes bankrupt, he can write off the entire amount!

Obviously, scale trading is not a system to pursue unless you want to guarantee yourself substandard returns peppered with an occasional financial disaster. In the next chapter we'll take this lemon of a method and make lemonade. By reversing the scale trader's tactics, we'll construct the Reverse Scale System, which will give us some small losses, some moderately large gains, and some huge gains that will make it all worthwhile. Better yet, the rules of this system will be as forthright and unambiguous as in the scale trading method.

THE REVERSE SCALE SYSTEM

The worst of all trading strategies systematically snowballs your losses and jettisons your best stocks just as they start to become winners. Practiced consistently, the scale-trading approach is a sure-fire ticket to the soup kitchen. The Reverse Scale System, on the other hand, is what results when you invert the trading rules of scale trading. It will deliver large profits over time. Before we get into the details of the Reverse Scale System, though, let's take a side trip to examine how all portfolios inevitably act over time.

THE ONE INEVITABLE CHARACTERISTIC OF ALL STOCK PORTFOLIOS

To begin with, let's think about a portfolio of 10 stocks held over a period of, say, five years. The only thing we know about the portfolio is that it is composed of 10 stocks. For now, let's not worry about which stocks are in the portfolio. What can we predict about the portfolio five years from now? In other words, what is certain to happen over the next five years?

We can't predict what the total return on the portfolio will be, because that will depend on market conditions over the next five years, and also on how well each of our 10 companies performs over the period. Stocks, on average, have historically returned about 9 percent per year, but over any five-year period this can range from a very negative number to a very positive one. And obviously we can't accurately predict what each individual stock in the portfolio will return, either.

Some people find it downright disheartening to realize how little we actually can foretell about the future performance of our portfolio, because their controlling fallacy is that prediction is the key to stock market profits. There is one thing we can say fairly confidently about what will happen with the basket of stocks we've chosen over five years, and it's this:

> **At the end of the five years, some stocks in the portfolio will have performed vastly better than others.**

This is not exactly a revelation. We could expect that one or two of the stocks will tremendously outperform the market averages, which might mean a move of two, four, or occasionally even 10 or more times our original entry price. Some will be dogs, perhaps declining only marginally or perhaps, in the extreme case, going out of business. Most of the stocks will have performed pretty much in line with the market: If you chose your stocks randomly, there's also a very good chance that your 10-stock portfolio will have returned something close to what the market averages returned over the five years. Since every portfolio of stocks contains future winners and future losers, we are left with this thought:

The challenge of investing is to make sure that when you get to the end of your holding period, most of your money will have been invested in the stocks that performed the best, and relatively little in the stocks that did the worst.

To realize how all this can be useful, we have to add another fact we've already discussed at great length:

Stocks make large moves in continuous trends, which almost always take months or years.

Large price movements are gradual, incremental events, not all-at-once step functions. They are evolutionary, not revolutionary. Whether the move is up or down, a really big move normally doesn't happen overnight—unless there's a merger announcement, a bankruptcy filing, an unexpectedly low earnings report, or something of that sort. Even then, the actual move has often been preceded by an uptrend (if there's a pending buyout) or a downtrend (if there's a likely bankruptcy filing). The reason is that there are always some folks who know about these issues before they happen, even if they aren't supposed to know. They're buying or selling just before a depressing announcement moves the stock while the public is still clueless.

So it's likely that there'll be a wide gap between the returns on the best-performing and on the worst-performing stock in your 10-stock portfolio. And the gap will widen *slowly,* but more or less steadily, as the holding period lengthens. Thus, there's only one logical conclusion:

If we could find a way to gradually allocate our investment dollars to the best-performing stocks in our portfolio as they are becoming the best-performing stocks, we'd have a tremendous chance to greatly increase our returns far beyond what would be achieved by simply choosing those same 10 stocks and holding them in equal dollar amounts.

REVERSING THE SCALE TRADING EXAMPLE

What we need, then, is a system that will systematically allocate capital to our strongest and best-performing stocks. As it turns out, we can do this simply by reversing the scale trading approach. So we add equal dollar amounts to our stock positions as they move up in price, instead of down. This is the key. In the rest of this chapter, you will see how the mathematics of this approach works greatly in our favor.

RICH MAN, POOR MAN

Since one picture is worth a thousand words, take a look at a price chart (Figure 10-1) of Home Depot for 1988 through early 1993. Let's compare the fortunes of two people who decided to invest in this stock, one using traditional scale trading, the other using the Reverse Scale System.

FIGURE 10-1: HOME DEPOT, 1988-1993

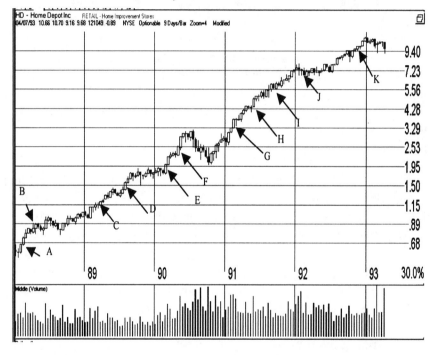

The scale trader is always looking for a decline to buy into with an initial position of $1,000. The Reverse Scale Trader instead is looking for a new high to buy into for his initial position of $1,000. Let's say both traders start to look into Home Depot in 1988 when it was trading below 68 cents per share (the actual share price was higher but has been adjusted for stock splits). The scale trader is waiting for a 30 percent decline; the Reverse Scale trader doesn't have to wait: A new annual high in price as his buy point occurs in 1988 at 68 cents per share (point A). The Reverse Scale trader will buy more shares at each subsequent 30 percent increase in price; he therefore buys additional $1,000 positions at points B, C, D, E, F, G, H, I, J, and K. The traditional scale trader never does get to buy any stock, because that elusive 30 percent decrease in price never occurs during this period.

As the stock of Home Depot ran upward, the poor traditional scale trader never made an investment, and therefore never had an opportunity to get one of his $300 profits. The Reverse Scale trader made 11 investments of $1,000 each ($11,000 total). When the price of Home Depot finally reached point K ($9.40/share), his $11,000 investment was worth roughly $56,000—a profit of $46,000.

The Reverse Scale trader owned other stocks at the time. He did not know Home Depot would be such an outstanding performer, but he didn't have to know. His system was designed to allocate the majority of his capital to the best-performing stock—exactly the opposite of the scale trader. The scale trader owned other stocks, too, and he was too busy buying more of the decliners in his portfolio to notice how much profit he was bypassing in Home Depot.

As you saw in the scale-trading example, no matter what happened, the scale trader's system gradually allocated most of his capital to the worst performing stocks, with a large loss the inevitable result. Like a snowball rolling downhill, the tendency for a declining stock is to keep on declining, and the tendency of the scale trader is to keep on losing. Once you really grasp how foolish the scale trading system is, it becomes much easier to see the merits of the Reverse Scale System. Table 10-2 will give you a flavor of the relative advantages of adding to a position as it moves up in price.

TABLE 10-2: THE ADVANTAGES OF THE REVERSE SCALE SYSTEM

Scale Trading	Reverse Scale System
Automatically allocates the majority of your money to your portfolio's worst performers.	Automatically allocates the majority of your money to your portfolio's best performers.
Unlimited potential for loss. There are an unlimited number of X percent declines between any positive number and zero.	Unlimited potential for gain. There are an unlimited number of X percent increases between any positive number and infinity.
Makes no attempt to cut losses. Adds to losing positions.	Cuts losses and lets profits compound themselves.

THE SNOWBALL EFFECT

Imagine you're standing at the top of a large hill. You've made five snowballs all the same size, and you give each of them an equal push to start them rolling downhill. One of the snowballs starts out okay but hits a rock that was hiding below the surface of the snow and explodes into pieces. Two others make it about halfway down the hill but then stall out because they got too big and happened to be on a part of the hill that wasn't as steep as some other areas. Still another makes it a bit further than those two but then gets bogged down in a wet area. The final snowball, however, happens to have just the right type of snow and a nice steep incline; its quick start, momentum, and, after a while, sheer size make it unstoppable. It goes several times farther than any of the other snowballs.

This is almost exactly what happens with a portfolio of stocks. Obviously, the snowball that rolls the farthest gets the biggest, picking up more snow gradually as it goes. A stock with momentum can be carried along by either losses or gains, depending on whether you're compounding losses with the scale trading approach or compounding gains with the Reverse Scale System. You have to choose the system.

With stocks, as with rolling snowballs, there are things you can control and things you can't. You can control how big you make each snowball, and you can control how much of a shove you give it. After that, many of the factors are not only unpredictable, even when they happen, they're out of your control. Even though we can't predict which snowball will roll the farthest, the hill still gives more snow to the one that eventually does go the furthest, because it adds snow gradually as the snowball progresses. The beauty of the Reverse Scale System is that just as the natural forces of the hill and gravity make sure the snowball that goes the farthest gathers the most snow, our system also makes sure that the stock that goes the farthest gathers not just most of our capital but also unusual amounts of profit.

The premise of both traditional scale trading and Reverse Scaling are the same: It is inevitable that at some point an investor will run into some runaway situations, and it's good to have a plan to get through them. But if you want to succeed in the stock market, you better have the right plan.

TRADING RULES FOR THE REVERSE SCALE SYSTEM: AN EXAMPLE

To learn how to implement the Reverse Scale System, let's run through an example for one stock. Although we will be using the system in a portfolio of a number of stocks, it's much easier to illustrate the concept using just one.

First, we construct a chart similar to what the hapless scale trader constructed, only our chart (see Figure 10-2) begins at the initial purchase price and goes up, each succeeding decision point being 50 percent higher than the previous one, rather than 50 percent lower, as with scale trading.

FIGURE 10-2: REVERSE SCALE SYSTEM CHART: AN EXAMPLE

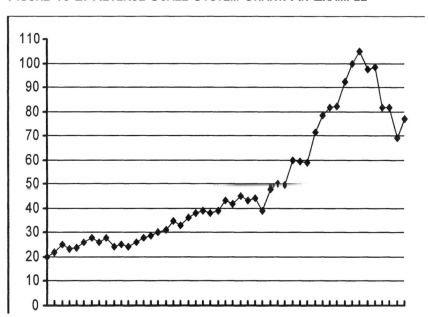

The basic trading rule is:

We will invest an additional designated number of dollars (we don't specify the number of shares) at each increasing decision point, but only if that level is reached.

As you can see, we will be adding a dollar amount at each price level that is equal to our initial position in dollars, but each time it will buy a reduced number of shares because the price is now higher. For a stock where our initial purchase was at $20 per share, our decision track would look like Table 10-3.

TABLE 10-3: REVERSE SCALE SYSTEM—
50 PERCENT PURCHASE INCREMENTS

	Decision Point Price	Amount Invested[2]	Shares Bought	Total Dollars Invested to Date	Shares Owned to Date	Current Value of Shares	Cost per Share	Average Total $ Profit/ (Loss)
Loss-cutting point	13.25	N/A	N/A	N/A	N/A	N/A	N/A	N/A
Initial entry point	20.00	$1,000	50	$1,000	50	$1,000	$20.00	$0
Decision point 1	30.00	$990	33	$1,990	83	$2,490	$23.98	$500
Decision point 2	45.00	$990	22	$2,980	105	$4,725	$28.38	$1,745
Decision point 3	67.50	$1,013	15	$3,993	120	$8,100	$33.27	$4,108
Decision point 4	101.25	$1,013	10	$5,005	130	$13,163	$38.50	$8,158

Each successive decision point is arrived at by multiplying the previous one by 1.5: 1.5 times the $20 initial entry price yields $30, the first decision point; 1.5 times $30 times is $45, and so on for as far as you need to go.

Our other basic trading rule is:

Whenever our stock reaches a decision point and then retreats all the way back to a previous decision point, we will sell out our entire position in the stock.

Why do we have this trading rule? Simple: If a stock retreats enough to make it all the way back to a previous decision point, it's highly likely that it's lost so much momentum that it will have a hard time becoming a market leader again—especially when the decision points are set this far apart (50 percent). In other words, its uptrend may be ending or it's about to go dormant for a long, long time. So trade it in and, if conditions are bullish, start over with another more promising issue, one that's both making new highs and fits the other criteria we laid out in Chapter 8.

---

[2]Since it's not possible to buy a partial share, this number doesn't always equal $1,000. It is the cost of the closest increment of one share that can be bought with $1,000.

Though we need to give a market-leading stock plenty of room for normal retreats off its highs so that we ride the long-term trends, we have to draw the line at some point. With decision points 50 percent apart, the prospect of "whipsaw" losses or prematurely bailing out of a stock are limited with this approach.

To illustrate, let's assume we took our initial position at $20 per share as indicated in Table 10-3. Over the next year, to our are delight, the stock increases in value gradually to $105 a share. We would have picked up shares at $30, $45, $67.50, and $101.25, for a total of 130 shares owned (see Table 10-4). Because the stock reached the decision point 4 at 101.25, our sell point would have ratcheted up to 67.50.

Let's say that the stock then retreats to the $67 range. When the stock violates our sell decision point 3 by falling below $67 1/2, we unhesitatingly enter a market order to sell the entire 130 shares. For the sake of simplicity, we'll also say we were able to sell our shares at exactly $67.50. The profit from the trade is shown in Table 10-4.

TABLE 10-4: SUMMARY OF PURCHASES

Purchase #	Shares Purchased	Price per Share	Total Cost	Commission	Net Cost
1	50	$20	$1.000	$25	$1,025
2	33	$30	$990	$25	$1,015
3	22	$45	$990	$25	$1,015
4	15	$67 1/2	$1,013	$25	$1,038
5	10	$101 1/4	$1,013	$25	$1,038
Total	130		$5,006	$125	$5,131

130 shares sold at $67.50 = $8,775
less $25 commission = $8,750.

Net Profit:
  $8,750
  -5,131
  $3,619

Just to illustrate the point about the Reverse Scale System making it hard to get shaken out of a stock prematurely, please note what our sell decision point would have been had the price topped out at only $100 instead of at $100.25 or higher. In that case, the price would have had to retreat from $100 all the way down to $45 a share to trigger a sellout, because it never reached $101.25 and therefore $67.50 never became our sellout point. Emotionally it might be frustrating to sit idly by while a stock sinks from a peak of $100 down to $45, but there are plenty of times where the discipline of being able to ride out the occasional temporary steep correction will be the very thing that allows you to sometimes go on to make a huge gain of 1,000 percent or more. And keep in mind that 1,000 percent gains happen much more often than you'd think if you use the stock-picking criteria presented in Chapter 8.

What would have happened if our stock had turned out to be a loser instead of a winner? If after we bought it at $20 a share, the stock declined to $13.25 ($20 divided by 1.5) or lower, we would have sold out and found a new stock to start over with, assuming market conditions were favorable (see Chapter 12 for more on determining market conditions). We would have lost $337.50 plus two $25 commissions, for a total loss of $387.50. We do not want to keep gunning for the same stock once we've been bumped out of it by our system.

Risk and Reward

While you might or might not be impressed with a profit of $3,619, keep in mind one other thing: We never exposed ourselves to a loss of more than $400 or so in this trade. With this system, while the potential for profit is theoretically unlimited (it's limited only by the performance of the stock being traded), the potential for loss is quite limited.

The power of the Reverse Scale System can be compounded by margin borrowing. So let's see how the Reverse Scale System can go hand in hand with the controlled use of borrowing to enhance the return on your portfolio. (We'll talk about implementation details and trading rules later.) We will end up with a portfolio management system that is approaching perfection in meeting the objectives of limited loss, limited personal cash investment, and unlimited profit potential.

Using Margin In the Reverse Scale System

As long as money has existed, risk-takers have multiplied their efforts by using other people's money. There is probably no place where the use of other people's money can be so effective in enhancing advantages (if you have a well-thought out plan) or speeding disaster (if you don't) as in the stock market. In real estate, for instance, you can borrow money, but there will be a banker there to make sure you don't make too bad a deal and thus put the bank's money in jeopardy, and a building he can take back if the deal does go bad. In the stock market there are few such safeguards. You can lose all of your money and a lot of someone else's if you aren't judicious in the use of debt.

Here's a quick review of margin trading before we go on. In stocks, you can easily borrow money using the value of the stocks you own as collateral. Current margin rules allow you to borrow to buy up to twice as much stock as you have cash in your account. By using margin, you now magically have the same number of dollars in your account, but more stock than you had before. This trading "on margin" always entails more risk than trading from a 100 percent cash position. Uncontrolled, it can be disastrous, considering that brokerage firms will lend you money to buy just about any listed stock, no matter how bad it is, and most NASDAQ stocks as well. You're free to get into as much trouble as you want. Lacking a plan to avoid trouble, many people get in far deeper than they realize.

If you decide to use margin, having an airtight plan and the discipline to follow it no matter what is doubly important. If you do have both of these elements you can obviously make a lot more money by trading on margin than by trading from a 100 percent cash position. If you don't have a plan and the discipline to follow it, you can lose a lot more money than you could on a cash-only basis. Be aware of the risks of margin as well as the potential.

The Reverse Scale System can be used with margin leverage while keeping the risk manageable. To effectively use margin, the first and most important rule is never borrow money to add more shares to a losing position. A losing position on anything is by definition trending downward at least from your entry point. We already concluded that we didn't want to buy into downtrending stocks even when trading from a cash position. We certainly don't want to *add* to any losing position, and with the ability of margin to magnify gains and losses we must be especially careful not to add to a losing position by borrowing.

The other thing to keep in mind is that while current regulations allow us to finance up to 50 percent of the value of the stocks we own, that much leverage is almost never a wise move. If you have a $20,000 account you can borrow from your broker to buy up to $40,000 worth of stock. This is a level of risk that will magnify gains and losses more than is tolerable for all but the most bullish of conditions. Using the maximum allowable amount of debt also means that if the position moves against you, you're likely to lose a huge amount of your equity in the part of the account you actually own.

We are not going to assume that much risk with our hard-earned money. Our rule for use of margin is this:

> **When we buy our initial position in a stock, we will always have enough cash on hand to make that purchase and half of our second purchase without borrowing anything.**

In Table 10-5, I've added two columns to Table 10-3 illustrating the Reverse Scale System—"Percent Financed" and "Cumulative Cash Deposited." Since each successive purchase is always $1,000 in value in this example, we deposit $1,000 to make the first purchase and $500 to make the second purchase. Our total cash deposited for this trade is therefore $1,500.

TABLE 10-5: USING MARGIN WITH THE REVERSE SCALE SYSTEM

Decision Point Price	Amount Invested	Shares Bought	Total Dollars Invested to Date	Shares Owned to Date	Current Value of Shares	Total Profit/ (Loss)	Total Borrowed	Percent Financed	Cumulative Cash Deposited
20	$1,000	50	$1,000	50	$1,000	$0	$0	0.0%	$1,000
30	$990	33	$1,990	83	$2,490	$500	$490	19.7%	$1,500
45	$990	22	$2,980	105	$4,725	$1,745	$1,480	31.3%	$1,500
67.50	$1,013	15	$3,993	120	$8,100	$4,108	$2,493	30.8%	$1,500
101.25	$1,013	10	$5,005	130	$13,163	$8,158	$3,505	26.6%	$1,500
151.88	$1,063	7	$6,068	137	$20,807	$14,739	$4,568	22.0%	$1,500
227.81	$911	4	$6,979	141	$32,122	$25,142	$5,479	17.1%	$1,500

The Cumulative Cash Deposited column shows that we would never have more than $1,500 of our own money on deposit. This column added to the Cumulative Dollars Invested column and the Total Profit/(Loss) column equals the Current Value of Shares column, because the current value of the stock we've invested in is composed of three elements:

1. The cash we've deposited (think of it as our down payment),

2. The amount we've borrowed from the broker, and

3. The accumulated profit we carry in the position.

Because the broker's regulation requires us to put up 50 percent of the value of the stock, we can use any unrealized gain as part of the 50 percent "down payment." This means that once we get to the third purchase and beyond, neither the broker's regulations nor our trading rule requires us to add any more of our own money to the trade, no matter how many more purchases the system requires us to make.

The Percent Financed column shows how much of the current value of stock we own is financed with borrowings from our broker. As you can see, at no time do we get even close to the 50 percent threshold, since the maximum borrowing we do tops out at 31.3 percent of security value as we add our third position. From then on, our profits snowball to such an extent that we are not required to add another dime of our own money to the trade for all purchases after the second one. Yet our percent financed declines for each position added after the third one.

The beauty of this approach is that when we lock onto a real winner, we can really pile onto the position without putting up much of our own money. From the table, you can see that if we execute our system on a stock that runs from $20 a share to $227.81, we will have an open profit of $25,142, less the interest paid on the borrowed portion, and commissions. Our total investment of our own cash was only $1,500 on the first trade. You may not find a stock like this every year, but inevitably you will if you stick with the Reverse Scale System and our stock-picking criteria. If you look at the Total Profit column, you'll see that you don't need anything even close to a tenfold move to make a large profit relative to the $1,500 of your own money invested.

We never start out using margin in the Reverse Scale System. Only after a stock has started to make a good run and our average cost per share is far below the market price, do we borrow to buy stock.

USING MARGIN IS NOT REQUIRED

The decision to use margin or not is yours alone. You can still use the Reverse Scale System without margin borrowing by simply ceasing to buy additional positions when you run out of cash. You can also buy just one position in each stock and leave it, never buying additional positions as the stocks rise in value. Even if you're not adding positions, though, you'll still want to track your stock's progress against the Decision Points, so that you'll know when to move your stop orders upward. In other words, whether or not you're adding to your positions, the decision points in the chart are useful for deciding when to sell out.

Obviously, the use of margin can make a big difference in your return. It works best during the most bullish of times. During less bullish times, you may be better off not adding shares as the decision points are reached. You need a large move to make money using margin and adding multiple buys of a stock. You need less of a move to break-even if you're not adding multiple buys. Table 10-6 shows how the profit picture would look if you simply took a $1,000 position and didn't add to it at all.

TABLE 10-6: REVERSE SCALE SYSTEM, NO MARGIN LEVERAGE

Decision Point Price	Amount Invested	Shares Bought	Total Dollars Invested to Date	Shares Owned to Date	Current Value of Shares	Total Profit/ (Loss)	Total Borrowed	Percent Financed	Cumulative Cash Deposited
20	$1,000	50	$1,000	50	$1,000	$0	$0	0.0%	$1,000
30	$0	0	$1,000	50	$1,500	$500	$0	0.0%	$1,000
45	$0	0	$1,000	50	$2,250	$1,250	$0	0.0%	$1,000
67.50	$0	0	$1,000	50	$3,375	$2,375	$0	0.0%	$1,000
101.25	$0	0	$1,000	50	$5,063	$4,063	$0	0.0%	$1,000
151.88	$0	0	$1,000	50	$7,594	$6,594	$0	0.0%	$1,000
227.81	$0	0	$1,000	50	$11,391	$10,391	$0	0.0%	$1,000

Using both Table 10-5 and Table 10-6, we can construct a comparison of the profit results of the same trade both with and without using margin leverage (Table 10-7).

TABLE 10-7: PROFIT COMPARISON OF MARGIN VERSUS NO MARGIN LEVERAGE

Price Level	Profit Using Margin	Profit Without Margin	Additional Profit from Margin
20	$0	$0	$0
30	$500	$500	$0
45	$1,745	$1,250	$495
67.50	$4,108	$2,375	$1,733
101.25	$8,158	$4,063	$4,095
151.88	$14,739	$6,594	$8,145
227.81	$25,142	$10,391	$14,751

So, if the stock moves from $20 to $227.81, the difference in profit is nearly $15,000, whereas the difference in our own dollars invested is only $500 (the $1,500 deposit in the margin example versus the $1,000 cash deposit in the non-margined example). For stock trends of smaller proportions, the differences aren't as huge but are still substantial. For short trends, you're better off not making additional buys at all. Using margin to make additional buys, you can make bigger profits on long trends but will make less money on short trends than if you'd just bought and held your initial position, moving your stops up as the decision points are reached. This is the essence of the tradeoff: There are always more short trends than long ones. However, eventually everyone using the stock-selection criteria in this book will lock onto some long, long trends.

Using margin is always more risky than not using it. Whatever you do to control the risk, you still own more shares than you would if you were trading without using borrowed money.

A major point repeated for clarity: If you're using the Reverse Scale System and not adding positions beyond your initial buy, you would still move your sell-stop up as the stock progressed through each succeeding decision point. In this case, the stop orders and decision points are a trend-following device, keeping you in sync with your particular stocks.

PRECAUTIONARY GUIDELINES

Some important principles to remember when using the Reverse Scale System:

1. Never spend more for a later position than you did for the first. If you bought $1,000 of stock at 20, never buy more than $1,000 of that stock in any single purchase. If you break this rule, you increase your average cost per share enough to practically guarantee yourself a loss at some point. You can, however, safely invest a lesser amount on subsequent purchases. For instance if your initial position were $10,000, it would be okay to systematically buy $5,000 more at each increasing decision point.

2. Only buy at decision points. Don't try to make "extra" buys between decision points. This is just another way of breaking the first rule and it leaves you exposed.

3. Never set your decision points closer than 50 percent above each other. If you do, normal market fluctuations can whipsaw you out, resulting in less profit and causing you to exit trends prematurely. You'll kick yourself as you watch your stock recover and start making new highs once again—without you.

4. Do not depart from these guidelines!

APPLYING THE REVERSE SCALE SYSTEM TO PORTFOLIOS OF STOCKS

Until now we've concentrated on how you make buy and sell decisions for just one stock at a time, because it's much easier to explain the concepts this way. But it's easy to adapt the Reverse Scale System to a portfolio environment because all we have to do is construct a separate decision chart for each stock in the portfolio and begin with an equal dollar amount in each stock. In the next chapter we'll review step by step how to use our system to accumulate and manage a portfolio of stocks.

When using the Reverse Scale System to manage a portfolio, always begin by investing the same amount in each stock. Don't try to guess which stocks will perform best, or you will defeat one of the key strengths of the Reverse Scale System, which is that we don't need to rely on prediction in order to profit.

DIVERSIFICATION

Let me say this again in no uncertain terms: Never invest a major amount of money in just one stock. It's risky because all your eggs are in one basket, and it's unnecessarily risky. If you have a number of stocks in your portfolio and use the Reverse Scale System, those few that perform exceptionally well will be added to as they progress upward in price. This will guarantee that eventually your best-performing stocks will make up a larger percentage of your portfolio than your poorer-performing ones. So you don't need to second-guess which stock will perform best beforehand.

If you're disciplined and follow the system, you will have the benefit of starting with a shotgun approach at the outset and progressing to more of a rifle approach as the market sorts out the winners for you. Ignoring principles of diversification and trying to guess which stock will do best decrease your chances of success.

In my opinion, you should never invest in less than five stocks to begin with, and that's the bare minimum. As a rule of thumb, aim to have at least 10 stocks in a Reverse Scale System portfolio. There's nothing magical about the number 10, but I feel it represents a good minimum if you're investing serious money.

The determinant of the minimum number of stocks you'll be owning should result from your loss control plan (Chapter 4), which is the starting point for any Reverse Scale portfolio. And that's where we'll start the example in Chapter 11.

DO NOT CHURN YOUR ACCOUNT!

Once you've chosen the stocks you'll trade, do not change stocks (selling one, buying another) unless the system tells you to. In other words, don't sell a stock unless it hits one decision point below the previously achieved decision point. Ever. If you depart from this system, you'll no doubt end up making emotional decisions, and they're likely to be poor ones. And you'll lose peace of mind because *you will no longer have a plan.* In short, you'll be right back where you were before you read this book.

A number of studies over the years have shown that excessive trading reduces investment results. The other name for excessive trading is *churning.* Whatever you call it, it's a waste of time and generally a tip-off that the investor doing it is confused about his system or is investing for excitement rather than profits.

If you resolve to use the Reverse Scale System, stick with it consistently. In the long run it will be the best policy.

GUIDELINES FOR PLACING ORDERS

MARKET ORDERS VERSUS LIMIT ORDERS

When you place an order you will be asked to specify if you want to execute your trade as a *market* order or as a *limit* order. *Always* use market orders, whether you're buying or selling. A market order specifies a willingness to buy at the current market price, whatever it may be. A limit order instructs the broker to buy at a specified price. A market order ensures that you will have your order filled, though the exact price is not guaranteed. A limit order guarantees that you will not pay a higher price than you specified, but does not guarantee that your order will be filled at all.

Bottom line: In real life, with the Reverse Scale System it's not critical that the order gets filled at exactly the prices listed in the decision chart. We're going after the big gains and a quarter or half-point variation won't matter much in the long run. It's much more important to get into the stock than it is to get a specific price.

STOP-LOSS ORDERS

If you don't already know about stop-loss orders, you should. They're commonly called just "stop orders." The order is placed below the market price if it's a sell stop order or above the market if it's a buy stop. If the stock's market price reaches the price specified in the stop order, then the stop order becomes a market order to buy or sell. Let's say we bought shares of ABC Co. at $20. They then rise to the first decision point price of $30 a share. We would then place a sell stop order for our shares at $20, which would instruct the broker to enter a market order to sell our shares *if and only* when the market price of ABC Co. again returns to $20 or below. If we enter it on a good till cancelled (GTC) basis, the order will stand until it's either triggered by the price reaching $20 or until we cancel the order. If you don't specify GTC, your order will be classified as a day order, meaning it will expire at the end of the day it's entered, so be careful to specify GTC on stop orders if you want them to last more than a day. Otherwise, you may have a false sense of security that your order is still entered when it really is not.

Currently, stop orders are available for both listed and NASDAQ stocks, a big change from just a few years ago, when they were only available on AMEX and NYSE issues. Since they are now so readily available, why not use them? They're a great convenience and can do the market-watching for you while you go about your other business.

If you can't watch the market during the day, I encourage you to use stop orders once you've accumulated a large position in a company's stock. The decision point parameters are set far enough apart with the Reverse Scale System that using intra-day prices (which is what stop orders are triggered by) or closing prices will not likely change your performance very much and may give you greater peace of mind.

Side note: Pay careful attention to your broker's policy on open order cancellation. Some firms, particularly discount brokers, will automatically cancel stop orders periodically on a preset schedule, without notifying you. This applies even to protective stop-loss orders on positions you're holding. How they could possibly think they're doing their clients a favor with this is beyond me, but just be aware of it and periodically check that all your positions are protected with stops.

APPLYING A LOSS CONTROL PLAN TO A PORTFOLIO

For the 10-stock $100,000 sample portfolio we've been using, let's put together a brief capital preservation plan, similar to the one in Chapter 4 but using the characteristics of our own hypothetical portfolio:

LOSS CONTROL PLAN

1. Account principal: $100,000

2. Maximum draw down tolerance percent: 15 percent

3. Maximum draw down tolerance (line one x line two): $15,000

4. Anticipated stop-loss percentage (Reverse Scale System): 33 percent

5. Maximum percent of account value to be risked on any one trade: 3 percent

6. Maximum $ value to be risked on any one trade (line one x line five): $3,000

7. Expected number of positions (line three ÷ line six): 5

8. Targeted size of positions (line six ÷ line four): $9,090

9. Total maximum amount to be invested: $45,450.

The 15 percent maximum drawdown tolerance (line two) is arbitrary and will vary from person to person. No one can tell you what this number should be, because only you can determine how much you are willing to risk. The same is true for line five, the maximum percent of account value to be risked on any one trade.

This plan tells us that with our stop-loss of 33 percent (standard on the Reverse Scale System), we could add up to five positions of roughly $9,000 each to achieve a maximum loss-exposure of 15 percent of the total capital available. Total investment allowed under this plan would be about $45,000 (line seven x line eight, rounded to $45,000). Naturally, since line six is the maximum loss per trade number, we could alternatively opt to invest in 10 positions of $4,500 each, which is what we'll be doing.

The intelligent investor keeps track of his total risk at all times. Roughly speaking, the total risk using our Reverse Scale System is the total, for all positions, of the current price minus the sell-stop price, times the number of shares. Table 10-8 shows the total-risk calculation for the sample portfolio we used earlier in the book, as it would have stood on April 22, 2002.

TABLE 10-8: TOTAL RISK CALCULATION FOR A SAMPLE PORTFOLIO

Symbol	Sell-Stop Price	Price April 22, 2002	Shares Owned	Current Price minus Sell-Stop	Total Risk
ASCA	22.31	33.46	200	11.15	$2,231
PENN	26.81	40.21	161	13.40	$2,158
ODSY	23.89	35.84	186	11.95	$2,222
LNY	17.70	26.55	245	8.85	$2,168
TRI	26.13	39.2	165	13.07	$2,156
PDX	31.89	47.84	135	15.95	$2,153
MAXF	4.80	7.2	924	2.40	$2,218
NBTY	12.80	19.2	340	6.40	$2,176
URBN	20.15	30.23	214	10.08	$2,156
COH	37.11	55.67	117	18.56	$2,171
Total Risk					**$21,809**

The total risk we're assuming (about $22,000) in our 10-stock port-folio exceeds the maximum amount allowed for in our loss control plan ($15,000). This could be corrected by reducing the initial position sizes from $6,500 to $4,500 each (to remain within the limits of the $45,000 amount to be invested).

The risk control plan needs to be calculated before taking any positions, a step we skipped earlier but one that should always be done before starting a Reverse Scale portfolio. The loss-control plan has its greatest value when you're just starting out. It makes you stare any potential losses in the face before you begin, something most investors rarely, if ever, do. Facing up to the risk you're exposing yourself to is enlightening and will lead you to responsible behavior, such as starting your investment process slowly and not taking positions that are too large. It's psychologically devastating to start off with a big loss; understanding the risks beforehand allows you to take precautions measures against that. The tendency for most investors is to take the largest position they can, and hope for the best. The combination of fear and greed then does its work, bringing on many bad decisions that result in a large loss. Taking a loss control (capital preservation) approach can help you to avoid this scenario.

Don't be too concerned if your loss control plan leads you to investing only a small portion of your account value, as in this example (45 percent), to start with. As some investments start to pull ahead of others, the amount you have invested will increase relative to the account value. If you keep pulling your stops up according to the system, your overall risk level (risk to your original principal) will not change, however.

CHAPTER SUMMARY

If you're a dedicated investor in individual stocks, eventually you'll have some "runaway" situations with stocks your own. Some will run away tremendously to the upside, some to the downside. What you need is a portfolio management system that capitalizes on the upside runaway situations and gets you out of the downside runaway situations.

Although traditional scale trading may sound appealing, it's a disastrous investment system. By reversing the trading rules of scale trading, we derive a portfolio management technique that limits our risk but capitalizes on large-scale stock trends. This system, the Reverse Scale System, has simple trading rules that you should know well before you begin to use it.

The Reverse Scale System can be used by adding positions to a stock as its price goes up, or it can be used simply as a capital allocation and trend-following device for determining when to raise our stops on positions we own.

If you decide to use margin with the Reverse Scale System, heed the position-sizing rules and your own loss control plan to avoid becoming overextended.

CHAPTER 11

IMPLEMENTING THE
REVERSE SCALE SYSTEM

Now that you have a good grounding in the Reverse-Scale System and in basic capital preservation concepts, let's review the steps you need to take to implement the system fully. Going through these steps the first time will take a while, but once you've done it you'll always know exactly when to buy and sell, and how much to buy or sell.

STEP ONE: DETERMINE HOW MUCH YOU CAN AFFORD TO COMMIT

All stock market investments have some risk, no matter what your approach to the market. Bear markets, national emergencies, and other unpredictable factors cause most stocks to decline temporarily. Because of the unpredictability of stock market performance over the short-term, it scarcely needs to be said that you should only invest capital that you will not need for at least a few years. You must establish exactly how much you can afford to commit to a longer-term system such as the one we've just outlined. How big will be your pool of risk capital? The term "risk capital" means different things depending on the psyche and risk tolerance of the investor; determining that number for you personally is outside the scope of this book. You alone must make the decision, but here are some things to consider when you do:

1. *Investment experience.* If you've never before traded stocks, start small until you're comfortable with the Reverse Scale System and you understand the mechanics and practices of stock trading. If you lack confidence, there's no use compounding your discomfort

by adding the stress of trading with too large a share of your money. You'll learn things as you trade that will give you confidence in handling larger amounts. Be patient. Give yourself time to learn before committing big money. Even with a small amount of available capital, you can still make a lot of money in the right conditions.

2. *Emergency planning.* If you aren't going to commit funds you'll need in the next five years, put them out of the way in an emergency fund. No one can rule out the possibility of a personal emergency over the next five years. Most financial experts recommend six months' living expenses, and I would consider that the minimum to put in your emergency fund.

3. *Age.* The older you are, the fewer years you have to weather the vicissitudes of the stock market. If you're only five or 10 years away from retirement, you may want to be a little more conservative in the amount of capital you put into an actively managed stock portfolio. More predictable investments may need to compose the majority of your holdings.

With these factors in mind, you need to take an honest look at your situation and assess just how much you want to commit to a longer-term investment program.

STEP TWO: CHOOSE AN APPROPRIATE BROKERAGE FIRM

There are several criteria against which to measure a prospective brokerage firm (1) commission structure, (2) insurance, and (3) attitude.

1. *Commissions.* Online brokerage firms charging as low as $5 to $12 per trade are now common, so it's virtually true that any size account can be profitably traded now. This is a great and very positive change from just a few years ago. At any rate, you should never have any problem keeping commissions down to 1 percent or less of the principal you're investing. As long as you do this, commissions will have no serious impact upon your results, using the Reverse Scale method.

2. *Insurance.* Make sure your brokerage account is insured for the full amount in case the firm holding your account should go bank-

rupt. Before you open an account, ask to see (in writing) what would happen if that should happen. The overwhelming majority of firms have adequate insurance through the Securities Investors Protection Corporation (SIPC) and private insurance contracts. But the opposite possibility still exists, and it's good to inquire about such things before committing your funds.

3. *Attitude.* Discount brokers are essentially order takers who offer no advice, which is precisely what we want and need. Even so, before you open an account it's good to call the firm's customer service department and ask a few questions, even if you have to make them up. You can learn a lot about the attitude of the brokerage firm and its employees by speaking with them personally. This is a good reality check on whether you can do business with them or whether there will be a clash between their culture and your personality. Of course, you also want to assess whether you can reach a live person easily, should you need to.

STEP THREE: CALCULATE YOUR LOSS CONTROL PLAN

This step is simple if you're not using margin. Once you've determined your maximum loss tolerance, simply use the format presented in Chapter 4 to construct the loss control plan for your account. This will tell you exactly how much to invest.

If you're using margin, it gets a bit more complicated. You still construct your loss control plan and determine how much to invest in your initial positions, but you need to choose the lower of either of the following:

1. The allowable investment level under your loss control plan, or

2. Sixty-five percent of your account value as the maximum amount you'll invest in all of your initial positions.

Where does the 65 percent come from? When you use margin, never buy initial positions totaling more than 65 percent of your account's value because you want to maintain enough cash in the account to pay for the initial position and half the next position without needing to borrow from the broker.

For example, in a previous chapter we constructed a loss control plan that told us we should invest only $45,000 of a $100,000 account in our initial positions to avoid losing more than we were comfortable with. Obviously, since 45 percent ($45,000 / $100,000) is lower than 65 percent, you would start by investing $45,000, not $65,000. The loss control plan takes priority over all other parameters, because it is the guiding plan that protects us from a larger-than-tolerable loss.

Let's begin to use the 10-stock portfolio we selected in Chapter 9. Let's also assume we have $100,000 in our sample trading account, but our loss control plan dictates that we invest no more than $45,000. We could split the $45,000 equally 10 ways and put $4,500 in each security. If we had a loss control plan that allowed for a large loss tolerance, we might have been able to invest $85,000, but we would still only invest $65,000, because it is the lower of the two numbers.

The reason we are using only 65 percent of our capital at first is that we want to abide by the margin-trading rule we developed previously:

> **To control leverage, we will choose our initial position size so that we will always have enough cash on hand to make our initial purchase and half of our second purchase without borrowing anything.**

Using no more than 65 percent of our capital for our initial positions in our 10 stocks ensures that we are complying with this part of our trading system. However, in this case our loss control plan had a lower number, so we go with that.

STEP FOUR: DECIDE WHICH ISSUES TO INVEST IN

We've already done this part in our example. Recall our manual effort to isolate 10 stocks in Chapter 9. We chose the 10 stocks over the weekend following trading on Friday, April 19, 2002. We entered orders over the weekend for the 10 stocks and on Monday morning received the opening prices shown in Table 11-1.

STEP FIVE: BUY YOUR INITIAL POSITIONS IN EACH STOCK

Calculate based on the most recent closing price how many shares you will buy in each issue. Don't worry that they aren't in even 100-lot quantities, which they almost certainly will not be. Instead concentrate on buying an equal dollar amount in each issue. In this case, we're taking initial positions of $4,500 in each company. Over the weekend, we would have placed orders and calculated the quantity based on the Friday closing price (rounding down to the next lowest whole number of shares).

TABLE 11-1: PRICES FOR INITIAL INVESTMENTS

Symbol	Closing Price on Friday, April 19, 2002	Opening Price on Monday, April 22, 2002
ASCA	32.42	33.46
PENN	40.20	40.21
ODSY	34.85	35.84
LNY	26.50	26.55
TRI	39.35	39.20
PDX	47.84	47.84
MAXF	7.03	7.20
NBTY	19.07	19.20
URBN	30.30	30.23
COH	55.42	55.67

Because there's a difference between the Friday closing price and the opening price on Monday morning, the actual initial positions will vary in value. As an example of what I'm talking about, consider ODSY (Table 11-2), which closed Friday at $34.85. We would have placed an order for 129 shares ($4,500 ÷ 34.85 = 129.12 shares), but when the market opened on Monday, our order was filled at the opening price of 35.84, so we actually bought $4,623 of stock (129 shares x 35.84 per share). Don't worry about the differences in position sizes created by the small changes in price that occur overnight. They generally will not have any material effect on our profits or system.

It's fairly typical for your initial order of uptrending stocks to cost more than you'd counted on. That's why we rounded down the number of share we were buying. We still exceeded the planned-for $45,000 initial position by $258, but the amount is immaterial to our plan, system, or results.

We can now construct our decision points based on our actual entry point for each stock, using the price per share actually paid for each position.

TABLE 11-2: ACTUAL COSTS OF INITIAL INVESTMENTS

Symbol	Closing Price on Friday, April 19, 2002	Opening Price on Mondy, April 22, 2002	Number Shares Ordered	Cost of Initial Positions
ASCA	32.42	33.46	138	4,617
PENN	40.20	40.21	111	4,463
ODSY	*34.85*	*35.84*	*129*	*4,623*
LNY	26.50	26.55	169	4,486
TRI	39.35	39.20	114	4,469
PDX	47.84	47.84	94	4,497
MAXF	7.03	7.20	640	4,608
NBTY	19.07	19.20	235	4,512
URBN	30.30	30.23	148	4,474
COH	55.42	55.67	81	4,509
Total				**45,258**

STEP SIX: CONSTRUCT YOUR ENTRY AND EXIT MATRIX PLAN

All that's necessary now is to finish filling out the Reverse-Scale System Decision Chart, as shown in Table 11-3. Here, we define the first few decision points (more can be added later, for stocks that make hefty advances) for each stock based on our initial entry point into that stock. The number of shares we acquire at each decision point can be penciled in as these acquisitions occur, as well as the total number of shares owned. For each stock individually, the sell point is always one level (33 percent) below the highest decision point reached (see Chapter 10). Once we have constructed this worksheet we can pencil in acquisitions as we go. Then we will know just by looking at the table what our current sell point is for each stock, as well as the next buy point. Table 11-3 shows how the chart would be filled out for our initial positions in the 10 stocks we picked out for our sample portfolio.

Each time a new higher decision point is reached, we will take a new $4,500 position and record the number of shares acquired. Adjust your stop order on the entire number of shares owned upward by one decision point. For instance, if NBTY reaches $28.80 a share, we would add 156 shares to our holdings ($4,500 ÷ 28.80 = 156, rounded downward), and adjust our stop order up to sell 391 shares (the initial 235 shares plus the 156 shares just purchased) at $19.20, on a good-till-cancelled stop order.

STEP SEVEN: MONITOR YOUR POSITIONS

These decision points are set far apart, so they won't be reached very ofen. This system is easiest to maintain if you:

1. Choose a broker that does not have a policy of canceling your GTC stop orders after a certain period.

2. Use GTC buy-stops to enter positions as well as sell-stops to liquidate them.

3. Choose a broker that pages you, calls you, or sends you an e-mail when your GTC orders are triggered and executed. This way, you can go about your life until something happens that warrants your attention.

TABLE 11-3: REVERSE SCALE SYSTEM DECISION POINT TABLE

Reverse scale started on: April 22, 2002
Initial and subsequent position amount: $4,500
50 percent scale

Symbol	Stop-Loss Price	Initial Entry Price	First Decision Point	Second Decision Point	Third Decision Point	Fourth Decision Point
ASCA	22.31	33.46	50.19	75.29	112.93	169.39
No. of shares:		138				
PENN	26.81	40.21	60.32	90.47	135.71	203.56
No. of shares:		111				
ODSY	23.89	35.84	53.76	80.64	120.96	181.44
No. of shares:		129				
LNY	17.70	26.55	39.83	59.74	89.61	134.41
No. of shares:		169				
TRI	26.13	39.20	58.80	88.20	132.30	198.45
No. of shares:		114				
PDX	31.89	47.84	71.76	107.64	161.46	242.19
No. of shares:		94				
MAXF	4.80	7.2	10.80	16.20	24.30	36.45
No. of shares:		640				
NBTY	12.80	19.20	28.80	43.20	64.80	97.20
No. of shares:		235				
URBN	20.15	30.23	45.35	68.02	102.03	153.04
No. of shares:		148				
COH	37.11	55.67	83.51	125.26	187.89	281.83
No. of shares:		81				

After we take our positions, it's pretty much a matter of waiting to see what happens next, as long as we have in place good-till-cancelled stop-loss orders for both buys and sells. They make life so much easier, why not use them?

STEP EIGHT: KNOW AND APPLY THE TRADING RULES

Eventually one or more of the stocks in your portfolio will reach the next decision point above where you got in or will decline below the previous decision point. In either case, you must take action. Thus, it is good to review the trading rules well so that you can apply them decisively.

> *Trading Rule One:* **Whenever a stock advances to a decision point not previously achieved, add a dollar amount to your position in that stock approximately equal to the dollar amount originally bought.**

For instance, we bought approximately $4,500 worth of PDX at $47.84, so if it rises to touch $71.76, we will add 62 shares ($4,500 divided by $71.76) to our position. We would update the PDX portion of our decision chart as follows:

PDX	31.89	47.84	71.76	107.64	161.46	242.19
No. of shares:		94	**62**			

No other stocks are affected by this change. We make decisions for each stock separately, based on the performance of *that stock alone.* Now that the chart has been updated, we can see all the information we need to know. We can see that the decision point of $71.76 has been reached, that we now own 156 shares, and that in order for us to sell our entire position PDX would have to decline to $47.84 or lower. We therefore make sure to put in a GTC sell-stop for 156 shares at a trigger price of $47.84. This scenario is covered in the next trading rule.

> *Trading Rule Two:* **Whenever a stock declines to the previous decision point, sell your entire position in that stock.**

If, instead of advancing, PDX had declined (without reaching 71.76 first) to as low as $31.89 after we took our initial position, we would have to sell out the initial position (94 shares) for a loss. There was never a signal to add to the position because it reached $31.89 before it got the opportunity to hit $71.76.

Once one of the sell points is reached, do not hesitate. Sell. Likewise, do not hesitate to buy whenever a new upward decision point is reached. Sometimes the best stocks rise very quickly, so it's crucial to act decisively, whether you're buying or selling. He who hesitates is lost. Or, has lost. If you believe in your plan, there is no reason to be hesitant. Using sell-stops and buy-stops means that your predetermined decision is executed before you ever get the chance to interject your emotions into the situation. Which is good.

> *Trading Rule Three:* **Once you've sold a stock, recommit the proceeds to a different stock (or stocks) than the one you've just sold—unless there's a bear market. To pick this new issue, use the same criteria you used to choose the original stock.**
>
> **If it's a bear market, do not recommit the money until conditions no longer fit the criteria for a bear market (see Chapter 12).**

Some people, once they've taken a loss on a stock, take it personally; they keep trying to "get even" with the stock by looking for an opportunity to buy it again. Don't fall into this trap. It's for ego-driven investors.

Forget the loss and the stock. If a stock has fallen far enough from its highs that it's now down at least 33 percent from the peak (the percentage difference between every decision point and its next lower decision point), it's probably entering a downtrend, and you don't want it. Take the money that's left and buy a different stock that's making new highs. Your money will be better employed and your account won't end up looking like the dog pound.

How do you know if you're in a bear market? It's all explained in Chapter 12, which deals with bear markets and how to recognize them; we'll defer discussion of that aspect of Trading Rule Three until then.

STEP NINE: PERIODIC ADJUSTMENTS

As the value of our account grows, we have to periodically adjust the size of the initial positions we take. For instance, if our $100,000 account equity grew to $225,000 and we sold one or two stocks, we might not want to take new initial positions as small as those we originally took. Instead of taking $4,500 initial positions, we might decide to take positions that are in proportion to our new account equity balance, in this case $10,125 ($225,000 ÷ $100,000 = 2.25, 2.25 x $4,500 = $10,125). With any successful investment plan, these types of adjustments need to be made as the amount of money you have to invest grows.

The other thing you could do is to stick with the $4,500 initial position size and simply work with a larger number of stocks. For diversification purposes and for simplicity, this is the preferred route to take.

The main thing is, don't overcommit yourself. When you sell a stock, don't invest more in new stocks than the proceeds from the one you sold. If you adhere to this rule, you'll never overcommit yourself.

HOW MANY STOCKS SHOULD YOU OWN?

Although our loss control plan tells us, based on our loss tolerance, how much money we can invest, it doesn't tell us how many stocks to buy with it. So how many stocks should you own?

The common wisdom says that the more stocks you own, the more closely your results start to mirror the broad market averages, such as the large-cap S&P-500 or, in the case of the portfolio of smaller-cap stocks we've selected in our sample portfolio, the small-cap Russell 2000 index. So, theoretically at least, the negative aspect of dividing your capital among a larger number of stocks is that you may be limiting your upside potential for the overall portfolio. However, there's less risk from any one security blowing up on you if you have 50 rather than five. In other words, the only way to get the potential for a high gain is by assuming a higher level of company-specific risk. Alas, there is no free lunch.

Here is why I disagree with the common wisdom, and why I tend to hold more stocks rather than fewer: I feel that when I hit upon a tenfold move, I will still be happy even if I own 20 stocks rather than 10 or five. After all, a tenfold move on 5 percent (that is, 1/20th) of your portfolio still gives you a return of 50 percent on the overall portfolio—not to mention gains realized from the other 95 percent of the portfolio. And that's just if you don't use margin or make additional purchases. Using the Reverse Scale System, a tenfold move on what started out as a $4,500 investment in our imaginary $100,000 portfolio (6.5 percent of total), results in a profit of roughly $213,000 on that part of the portfolio alone. With 20 stocks or more, I stand a better chance of bagging one of these large profits, by virtue of the fact that I have 20 chances to do so, not five or 10. Plus, I get the added comfort, and the cushion, of having a more diversified portfolio.

If you're playing the universe of low-priced stocks looking for a windfall, you need to diversify over a large number of stocks (at least 20) to have things work out. The attrition rate is high in this category. That's why I don't recommend that you devote more than 20 percent of your individual stock portfolio to low-priced shares (and I don't recommend that you devote any of your portfolio to stocks trading below $5). Yet I also understand that inevitably, someone out there will not heed this advice, so I recommend that you hold at least 20 low-priced stocks if you decide to use this system.

Whatever type of stock you hold, always place a sell-stop when you buy a stock, and adhere to our other trading rules at all times.

CHAPTER SUMMARY

This chapter summarizes the nine steps to take in implementing the Reverse Scale System. Be sure you understand them all before proceeding. Adhere to both the margin-trading rule of not committing more than 65 percent of your account value in your initial positions, and also adhere to your own loss control plan.

CHAPTER 12

BEAR MARKETS: HOW TO AVOID TRADING AWAY YOUR PROFITS

In any trading system, the most important thing is to preserve your capital. Capital preservation is all-important because if you seriously deplete your trading capital, it becomes very difficult to get back even to where you started out, much less make a profit, because you're then working with a smaller amount of capital.

The two main sources of capital depletion are from whipsaw losses (rapid-fire in-and-out trading, which almost always results in lots of small loooooo, a few small gains, and large commission expenses) and from failing to cut losses on poor investments. The Reverse Scale System already has many capital-preserving mechanisms built into it. Among these are diversification among many securities, the loss-cutting decision rules, and the fact that we don't add to positions until they're showing us a good profit. Also, our decision points are set far enough apart (50 percent) so that whipsaw losses are extremely unlikely, especially with stocks selling for more than $15 per share. In addition to these measures, we now know that even before we invest a dime, we should draw up our own loss control plan.

The one remaining factor we need to address is bear markets and how to behave during them. All our loss control measures up to this point have addressed some issues tangential to bear markets but we need to address the phenomenon directly, because bear markets have a profound effect on market behavior—and on our ability to make a profit.

HOW TO AVOID CAPITAL DEPLETION DURING BEAR MARKETS

The worst thing about bear markets is the possibility of several losses coming in quick succession. Because bear markets are not only inevitable, they're unpredictable, we need to add Trading Rule Four to ensure that we can survive those inevitable times when the market goes down for an extended period, pulling almost all stocks down with it.

> *Trading Rule Four:* **Assume you're in a bear market if the 50-day MA for the S&P 500 index is lower than the 200-day MA. Don't buy any new stock until the 50-day rises above the 200-day MA.**

Always observe this rule. Do *not* make exceptions!

Make careful note that you do not want to start a Reverse Scale portfolio when the 50-day moving average line is below the 200-day moving average, either. You should not be buying any positions in new stocks while the 50-day is below the 200-day.

The purpose of Trading Rule Four is to force us to wait until the market as a whole is showing signs of positive momentum before we commit funds. In other words, we do not want to get into a situation where we are buying new stock, selling it for a loss, using the proceeds to buy yet another new stock, and then being forced to sell that one for a loss, too. This could happen during very severe market downturns. Your portfolio cannot sustain multiple successive 33 percent losses in any of its positions, and there is no reason to endure this, anyway. That's why it's a good idea to wait until the market has shown some strength before committing funds to a new position. Your win to loss ratio will be much better if you observe this rule. And if you don't observe it, eventually your portfolio will be destroyed.

Most of the time, the 50-day moving average will be above the 200-day moving average. However, when conditions are bearish, the situation reverses. These conditions can sometimes last for a long, long time. Most of your positions will decline; in fact, most of your positions will meet their sell points and you will be forced out of them. Expect this. It will happen. However, if you observe Trading Rule Four, you will survive with a great deal of profit.

Of course, if you started this program at the top of the market cycle, and recklessly plunged in all at once rather than starting slowly (as is strongly recommended), you will probably lose the maximum amount allowed under your loss control plan—but, even then, you'll be a lot better off than if you kept entering successive new positions only to be knocked out of them at a loss. Wait until better conditions exist, and you'll be much more successful.

Of course, it goes without saying that any stock you eventually pick for reinvestment needs to be chosen using the criteria from Chapter 8.

REALITY CHECK

This is an opportune point to remind you (as I did in Chapter 9) that our imaginary 10-stock portfolio would not have been purchased in real-life conditions. Why? Because as of April 22, 2002, the 50-day moving average was still below the 200-day MA for the S&P 500 index. Trading Rules Three and Four also apply to beginning a Reverse Scale portfolio: Don't begin the investment process unless the market is in bullish territory as defined in Trading Rule Four.

HOW TO MONITOR THE 50- AND 200-DAY MOVING AVERAGES

Those two moving averages are very easy to monitor via the Internet. A couple of good sites to visit would be *StockCharts.com* or *BigCharts.com*. Both have interactive charting abilities so you can specify the moving averages you'd like to see plotted. Simply choose 200- and 50-day as the averages of choice. *StockCharts.com* has the advantages of having these two averages as the default selection, and it actually shows you the values of each, which eliminates the need to make judgments about whether or not the two lines have crossed.

CLARIFICATION

Don't sell any of your positions simply because the 50-day average may have fallen below the 200-day line. In other words, don't adjust stop orders upward simply because the 50-day MA on the S&P 500 has moved below the 200-day MA. We use Trading Rule Four only to help us determine when, or if, to add new positions. Our stop orders alone are what determine when we sell out a position. Hence, you may be holding positions when "officially" in bear territory, but you wont' be adding any new ones, or replacing ones that were sold unless at least one of the indexes is above the line.

EMERGING FROM BEARISH CONDITIONS

Once the 50-day again exceeds the 200-day MA on the S&P 500, you will still be well served to go slow in adding positions. Don't recommit all your cash at once the moment the indexes enter positive territory. In fact, you stand a much better chance of preserving your capital and achieving eventual success if you add new positions very slowly. There are two reasons for this (1) time-based diversification and (2) sector rotations.

TIME-BASED DIVERSIFICATION

In addition to the diversification we achieve by holding a number of stocks in our portfolio and by diversifying among asset classes (stocks, bonds, real estate, etc.), we can add another dimension of diversification to our portfolio of individual stocks. We can practice time-based diversification, where we begin the Reverse Scale System slowly, rather than by building a portfolio of, say, 10 stocks all at one time.

Investment approaches that emphasize entering the market or exiting the market all at once are riskier than they need to be. You'll have much more confidence in the Reverse Scale System if you get off to a profitable start, and you'll have a better chance of a profitable start if you don't invest all your money at once. The main reasons people do enter the market all at once are generally fear, greed, or lack of understanding. None of these are good reasons, clearly. Wanting to make an extreme killing or fear of being left behind in a runaway bull market are the typical emotional precursors to plunging in all at once.

There are many ways to enter the market slowly using the Reverse-Scale System. A few options are:

1. Buy one position per month for 10 months (for a 10-stock portfolio).

2. Buy three positions every quarter.

3. Hold more, smaller positions and add one more often.

Be creative. There are lots of ways to begin the process, and no one right way. In fact, there's a lot less pressure when you begin slowly than when you begin fully invested.

Starting a Reverse Scale portfolio gradually accomplishes two things (1) it reduces your chances of entering the market at just the wrong time, and (2) it reduces your chances of entering the market at just the right time. People jump in because they imagine they're going to miss something wonderful, but frankly, wonderful things don't happen so often that you're likely to miss them altogether by working patiently. If you survive in the short-term by beginning the investment process gradually, eventually you'll be there when something wonderful does happen.

SECTOR ROTATION

The other reason for entering the market slowly is because of the sector rotation that takes place during bear markets and early in bull markets. Sector rotation is when market leadership (the industries experiencing the largest percentage price gains) moves from one industry to another.

When a bull market is just beginning, certain industries lead the way. Then, just as they seem to be getting started, those industries go dormant or even take a nasty crash as another set of industries takes their place. A former leading industry may or may not resume leadership. It may even enter a downtrend. This process generally becomes less severe as the bull market matures and the true leaders of the market emerge. If you enter the market all at once before the market has finally sorted out the industries that will lead to new heights, you can end up with lower performance than if you had entered slowly and gradually accumulated positions as the bull market matured.

Sector rotation is another reason we wait until the S&P's 50-day exceeds its 200-day MA: By the time this happens, the market has had time to mature and sort out the final leading industries. Much of the "thrashing and crashing" between industries is over. By waiting, we're more likely to avoid buying prematurely into industries that appear to be the emerging leaders, but aren't going to be the ultimate leaders once things really get going.

A COMMON MISTAKE

If you decide to work your way into the Reverse Scale process over time instead of all at once, make sure you perform a new criteria search for stocks each time you are buying stock. In other words, don't identify 10 issues that meet all the criteria in June, buy one of them then, and then a month later go back to the same list because you're now ready to buy a different position! Candidate lists grow stale in a day or two, so you must start the search process with a clean sheet of paper every time you want to add a new position.

Let's take our 10-stock portfolio as an example. Imagine we decided to buy just one, the highest-ranking stock, per month instead of buying all 10 at once. Our highest-ranking stock (the one with the highest growth factor ranking) on April 19, 2002 was ASCA. We buy our $4,500 initial position in ASCA when the market opens on Monday, April 22. One month later, when we go to buy another stock, we start with the new-highs list for May 20, 2002 and again apply all our screening criteria. We wouldn't use the list generated from April 19 to select a buy candidate in May.

PRECURSORS TO BEAR MARKETS

There's no objective indicator of bearish conditions that's foolproof. All give false signals, so there always is risk in following these signals. Trading Rule Four is no exception. It will at times cause you to stand aside while the market zooms ahead and at other times allow you to invest just before a downtrend starts. However, the fact is that during the majority of a bear market, it will keep you out. It's also true that during the majority of a bull market, you will be in synch with the market's trend. Hence, while observing this rule doesn't get you in at the bottom and out at the very top, it does keep you out of the market while most of the damage is being done (see Table 12-1).

TABLE 12-1: HOW TRADING RULE FOUR PERFORMED DURING SOME NOTABLE BEAR MARKETS

Bear Market	S&P 500 Index at Market Top	S&P 500 Index at Market Bottom	Trading Rule #4 Triggered	Market Decline Avoided
1969-70	109.37	68.61	97.32	70%
1973-75	121.74	60.96	111.57	83%
1981-82	141.96	101.44	128.64	67%
2000-01	1552.87	944.75	1398.00	75%

OTHER BEAR MARKET OMENS

In addition to those times when Trading Rule Four says that conditions are unfavorable for taking new positions, there may be other times when you might want to be on your guard. Let's briefly review other precursors to the onset of a bear market, so that you can learn to be aware of them and perhaps sidestep disaster.

In addition to market momentum (covered by Trading Rules Three and Four), the main additional precursors to bear markets are (1) an inverted yield curve, (2) rising interest rates, (3) implosions of leading stocks, and (4) angry reactions to good sense.

YIELD CURVE INVERSION

An *inverted yield* curve is often a precursor to the onset of a bear market. Although it sounds complex, rate inversion is simply a situation where market rates of interest for short-term U.S. government securities are higher than market rates for longer-term securities of the same credit quality. The normal state of affairs in the debt markets is that short-term instruments yield less than longer-term instruments because it's assumed that investors prefer maximum liquidity. When the reverse is true, it says that the debt markets sense a coming slowdown in business activity, a more accommodating Federal Reserve Board, lower demand for capital, and hence lower rates ahead.

The debt markets are frankly more efficient and more objective than the stock market, being far less prone to manias and fads. As a result, when the debt markets warn of a slowdown ahead, we do well to listen.

An inverted yield curve doesn't happen very often, which is another excellent reason to heed its warnings. From the early 1990s to early 2002, the yield curve inverted only twice. The first time was in September 1998 during the Asian financial crisis. The debt markets expected the Asian situation to slow the U.S. economy down. Fortunately, it didn't have the profound effect that was expected. The debt markets were only fooled for a very short time—this inversion lasted only a month. The second one was in late August/early September 2000, just as the market as measured by the S&P 500 index was peaking before the onset of the bear market of 2000-2001. This inversion lasted until roughly March 2001. In both cases, rates on five-year Treasuries were lower than 90-day T-bills.

So the track record of inverted yield curves is fairly good, even in recent history. Not perfect, but good. Unlike the boy in the fable, the yield curve doesn't cry "wolf" very often, so when it does, heed its warning.

The best way to keep aware of the current condition of the yield curve is to subscribe to the *Wall Street Journal, Investor's Business Daily,* or another publication that carries the yield curve regularly. Or you can just use your local newspaper to occasionally compare the yields on 90-day, five-year, and 30-year Treasury securities. If you see the rates for the longer maturities coming into line with, or undercutting the shorter-term rates, beware.

RISING RATES

Rising interest rates are death to stocks. Future earnings are discounted to present value at a higher discount rate, causing the present values of most securities (stocks and debt instruments) to fall. In addition, rising rates can cause future economic activity to fall, impacting the outlook for earnings. This one-two punch leaves stocks reeling with anticipation of bad times to come.

Except for inflation-induced rate increases (which usually have an immediate negative impact on the market), it normally takes a year or longer for rising rates to derail a bull market. Sometimes rates stop rising before the bull market's back is broken, but if they don't and continue to increase, sooner or later the market will suffer.

When you see the Federal Reserve raising the federal discount rate, that's evidence that bear market risk factors are starting to pile up.

IMPLOSIONS OF LEADING STOCKS

When you notice regularly that stocks that had been in protracted uptrends start morning trading with "gap-down" openings of five, 10, or more points (15-50 percent overnight losses), this is a very bad sign that a current bull market is ending. Corrections within uptrends are normal, but mere corrections normally don't exhibit gap-down openings for leading stocks. And, if you start to see this phenomenon almost every day, watch out—the foundation of the market is starting to crack.

If you're on the receiving end of one of these implosions, it is not fun. However, one of the reasons we set our decision points so far apart in the Reverse Scale System is that once we've bought several quantities of a stock, our average price per share is well below the current market price. So while it may not feel good to have one of your stocks crash, the damage to your principal should not be devastating.

Angry Reactions to Good Sense

One of the most subjective but reliable signs that the market may be getting into turbulent waters is, believe it or not, anger. Preceding the several bear markets I've experienced, I and others have been met with unwarranted hostility simply for suggesting normal precautions like placing sell-stop orders or diversifying among asset classes.

The typical situation is this: The investor you're speaking with happens to be convinced a certain company or industry is so good, so flawless in every respect, that it should be held forever. If you mention placing a sell-stop order just in case something unforeseen happens, the reaction ranges from dismissal to outright hostility. "Yes," the investor may concede, "placing a stop-order is a good practice, but you don't understand—this company is the exception. It's going much higher and if it should go lower for a bit, that's merely a buying opportunity." It quickly becomes apparent that nothing but a big, fat loss will ever convince this person that he has not really found the epitome of businesses.

When you start to get suggestions that you should undergo psychiatric counseling because you don't own a certain stock, or because you don't have all your money invested in a particular sector, take it as a strong warning. This is one of those rare moments when contrarian thinking is appropriate. Take it as another sign that you might want to delay adding new positions or other purchases of stock, if some of your positions are being stopped-out.

If you see these precursors to a bear market, let cash build up in your account as your positions are liquidated. And needless to say, you certainly should be letting cash build up in your account if Trading Rule Four says you're in a bear market.

Chapter Summary

Never start a Reverse Scale portfolio when you're in a bear market as defined by Trading Rule Four. Also, never add new positions to your Reverse Scale portfolio when conditions are bearish as defined by Trading Rule Four. As you are stopped out of positions, let cash build up in your account as long as the 50-day MA is below the 200-day MA. This has a good track record of keeping assets safely out during most of a bear market.

Also learn to recognize other signs of impending bear market conditions. These can be useful for making more subjective decisions about how cautious to be in entering new positions.

SECTION IV
OPTIONAL PRECISION TIMING TACTICS

CHAPTER 13

USING CHARTS TO IDENTIFY
PRECISION ENTRY POINTS

This section is included for those who may want to learn to use charts to identify precise entry points when first entering a new position. It's also included for those who may want to use charts to more selectively identify potential large gainers. Both are optional. The Reverse Scale System may be implemented successfully using only the information presented thus far.

The use of precision entry tactics is definitely more time-consuming and requires more trading activity than simply using the system as defined in Chapters 10 through 12. The advantage is that you can enter stocks at critical trading points, and you can cut losses very quickly and for a much smaller percentage loss when your selection or timing may be wrong.

Even for those who don't want to be bothered with precision entry techniques, the section in this chapter on elephant hunting may still be useful for identifying high-potential winners and doesn't require the use of precision entry.

Let me state this explicitly: The tactics outlined here are for use only with stocks that are near their high price for the year and also meet our other criteria for stock selection. When using precision entry tactics, most of the time you will be buying stocks not when they're making new highs but when they're slightly (at most 15 percent) below their highs for the year. It should also go without saying that these techniques should not be used when the market is bearish (see Trading Rule Four).

PROPER USE OF CHARTS

ARITHMETIC SCALE VERSUS LOG SCALE

I like to use stock charts that use a logarithmic rather than an arithmetic scale. On a log-scale chart, a percentage move of 10 percent is the same distance at any place on the chart, but on an arithmetic scale, a percentage move of 10 percent at a low price will seem very small and at a higher price will seem very large. Compare the two charts shown in Figures 13-1 and 13-2, which cover the exact same stock and time frame.

FIGURE 13-1: ARITHMETIC SCALE

As you can see, the log-scale chart has the following advantages over the arithmetic scale chart:

    1. It shows that the stock price is appreciating steadily, whereas the arithmetic scale chart gives the impression of an ever-increasing rate of growth.

FIGURE 13-2: LOGARITHMIC SCALE

2. The arithmetic scale loses all the detail of the stock's earlier price action.

The log-scale chart is much better at giving us a true picture of the trend and the price action in previous periods. Use log-scale not arithmetic-scale charts when you analyze the price action of a stock.

THE COMPOSITION OF UPWARD TRENDS

Before you can recognize precision entry points, you need to understand the basic composition of stock trends. As most of us know, stocks don't advance in a straight line. A price trend is a combination of the following stages, repeated endlessly:

1. *Advance.* The stock makes a largely uninterrupted move upward, generally between five percent and 30 percent, over a number of days.

2. *Correction.* A minor pullback in the price does not completely offset the previous advance. It's usually characterized by a series of

days where most successive intra-day high prices don't violate the intra-day high of the previous day. It generally ends after two, or more, often three or more days of price action where the intra-day highs of each successive day are lower than the previous day's high price. The correction phase ends with either an abrupt upside violation of the previous day's high, closing higher than on the previous day or a gradual leveling-off where each successive day's high price is lower than the previous day's high price but by an ever-decreasing amount. In the case of a leveling-off resolution, the previous day's high is violated on a closing basis, but may not be an abrupt violation, with more significant advances in price and volume taking place several days later.

3. *Consolidation.* After several advance and correction phases, the stock does several back and forth trips within a narrowing trading range as it digests the collective advance and correction phases. This phase may or may not precede another set of advances. If it is to be resolved to the upside, it usually does this in one of several ways covered in the next section.

These three phases appear in every upward stock trend, although sometimes a phase is obscured by the erratic trading tendencies of a particular stock. Because each stock has its own personality, the phases will take on a slightly different form for each. It's usually easier to recognize the phases for smaller-cap stocks; the phrases for the large-cap, institutional favorites are often more erratic as the institutions trading feed on one another. Figure 13-3 shows a stock trend with the phases identified. You may want to make careful note of how the correction phases often (but not always) end with three or more days of successively lower intra-day highs. This fact can help you anticipate the resumption of the uptrend.

In the correction phases in the example in Figure 13-3, note the number of times there are clusters of two, three, or more days where each day's intra-day high is lower than the previous day's. We will use this phenomenon in the next section on precision entry points.

PRECISION ENTRY

The point of learning precision entry points is not primarily to identify an area where a stock will begin a major advance—that's actually just a side

FIGURE 13-3: STOCK TREND PHASES

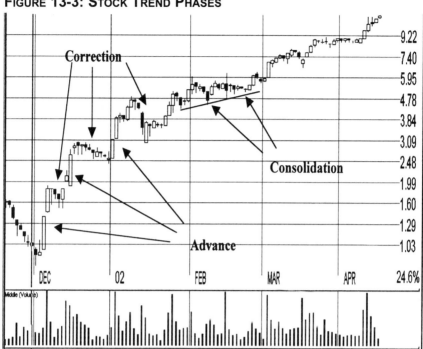

benefit of precision entry. The real point is that these techniques give us a place to enter a stock where we can limit our losses (should the trade fail) to a very minuscule percentage. Sometimes, the stock we buy at a precision entry point will move only very slightly (five to 20 percent) in the first few days or even weeks. After what is happening becomes obvious to others, the advance starts to pick up volume and the price increases at an accelerated rate. The first objective here is loss limitation, and the secondary goal is a steady advance afterward. It is not necessary that we get into the stock one day before it blasts off, only that we get into the stock, have it advance moderately while limiting our downside risk, and still own the stock when it does blast off.

THE TWO MAJOR PRECISION ENTRY TECHNIQUES

THE DESCENDING-HIGHS TECHNIQUE

Within the correction phases of advances (and even within trading ranges), there generally will come a series of days where each successive day's intra-day high does not significantly exceed (if it exceeds at all) the *intra-day high* of the day immediately preceding it. This observation, noted in the section on the Composition of Upward Trends, is the basis for this technique. After several such days, as few as two or possibly as many as 10, there comes a day when the price rises above the previous day's high, which sets the stage for a rally attempt. It is at this point that the informed investor buys the stock, setting her sell stop-loss order at a level below the lower of yesterday or today's intra-day low. Consider the very common example shown in Figure 13-4.

FIGURE 13-4: DESCENDING HIGHS: EXAMPLE ONE

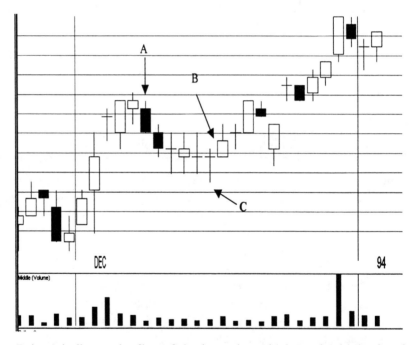

Point A indicates the first of six days where the intra-day high of each day is lower than the high of the previous day. Point B indicates where the savvy investor would place a buy-stop order, just slightly above the preceding day's high. After the buy-stop order is triggered at point B (that is, where the previous day's high is exceeded), the investor places a protective sell-stop at point C, just under the previous day's intra-day low, to protect against reversal. Generally, the first day where the previous intra-day high is exceeded will also show an increase in trading volume over the previous day. If not, the success of the trade may be questionable.

Figure 13-5 may help you develop the skill of spotting the descending highs opportunity.

FIGURE 13-5: DESCENDING HIGHS: EXAMPLE TWO

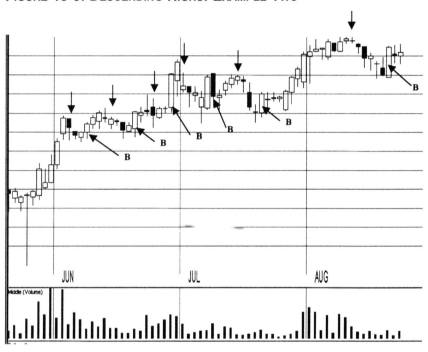

This real-life trend illustrates how the descending-highs technique can be used fairly often to enter an advancing stock with limited risk. In this instance, in the course of three months the descending-highs phenomenon presented itself at least six times. The stock went on to a much larger gain. The downward pointing arrows indicate the beginning of a series in which the intra-day highs began descending and the points marked "B" indicate where the previous intra-day high was violated (the buy point). In each case, the investor could have placed a sell-stop under the previous day's low and at no point would any of the six sell-stops have been triggered during this advance. If you look through charts every day, you soon get to the point where spotting these opportunities is sec-

ond nature. There is more in the next section on how to use this technique
to enter stocks as they form consolidations.

VOLUME CLUES

Once again, it's useful to note that a violation of the previous day's high
within the context of a descending-highs pattern is often accompanied by
an increase in volume over the previous day. The increases may or may
not be large, but there should be some increase. The increase in volume
doesn't have to be above the stock's average daily trading volume, but
only above the volume for the previous day. In the example shown in
Figure 13-5, only one of the six descending-highs patterns (the first one)
did not have this increase in volume. Truly large increases in volume
often don't occur until several days later, when the rest of the world starts
to notice the rally.

THE RESISTANCE-VIOLATION TECHNIQUE

The resistance-violation technique involves buying a stock once it trades
above an identified line of price resistance—what in recent years has
become known as a "breakout." In certain cases, it isn't possible to identify descending highs (particularly with the largest-cap stocks), and so
instead we must buy when the consolidation is completed. This doesn't
happen too often, as most stock consolidations do present descending
highs that can be capitalized on for a limited-risk entry somewhere within the consolidation. Figure 13-6 is an example of such a situation.

Although we could have bought using the descending-highs technique in the third week of November and possibly one or two other times,
assume for the sake of discussion that we did not. As an alternative, we
could buy on the violation of the line of resistance in the early part of
January. Once the line of resistance is violated and we bought, we would,
as with the descending-highs technique, place a sell-stop order at point A,
just under the previous day's low. (Of course, you can always buy when
the stock completes the consolidation and pops up to new highs, but then
you'll be buying when everyone else is buying, subjecting yourself to a
greater risk of a whipsaw reversal and exposing yourself to a greater
potential percentage loss as well.)

FIGURE 13-6: RESISTANCE VIOLATION

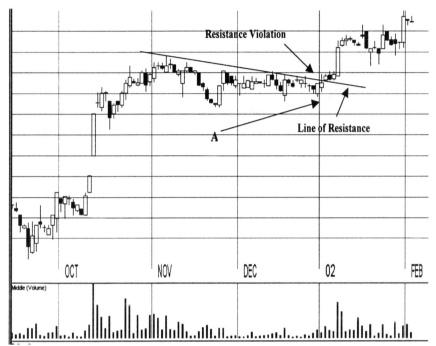

HOW TO USE MAJOR PRICE CONSOLIDATION PATTERNS FOR PRECISION ENTRY

Consolidations are significant because they are often a precursor to higher prices. They usually occur when a price advance has gotten ahead of itself and the stock needs to mark time while the previous sustainable trendline "catches up," so to speak. Most consolidations consist of one or more advance and correction phases, often complete with descending highs and violation of those highs, while the stock moves within a trading range. Normally this range, and the advance and correction phases within it, becomes narrower as time goes on, ultimately culminating in a resolution of the consolidation, hopefully to the upside.

FLAT-TOP AND DECLINING CONSOLIDATIONS

The two most common consolidation patterns are the flat-top pattern shown in Figure 13-7 and the declining pattern shown in Figure 13-8.

FIGURE 13-7: FLAT-TOP CONSOLIDATION

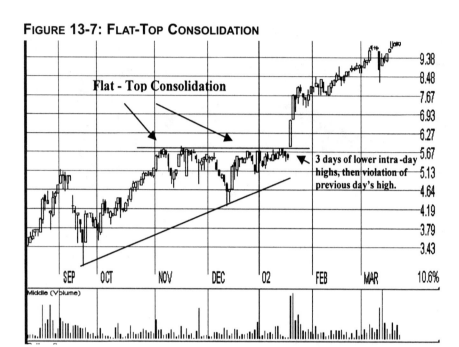

FIGURE 13-8: DECLINING CONSOLIDATION

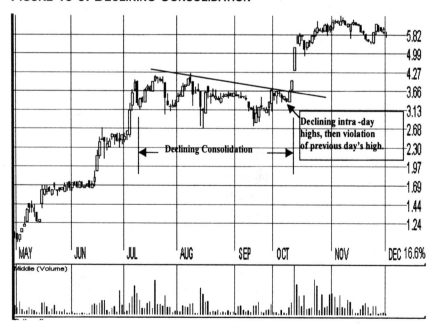

In these patterns, there generally is a line of resistance that develops to contain the upside of the stock as the consolidation phase is building. Although we have so far talked only about buying stocks that appear on the 52-week high list, most of the time an advance from a consolidation does not begin at a new high in price but within the extremes of the consolidation—so when using precision entry points you will usually be buying at a price slightly lower than a new 52-week price high. As was noted in the section on the Composition of Upward Trends, correction phases generally end after a series of days where each day's intra-day high is lower (or possibly equal to) the previous day's high.

PARABOLIC CONSOLIDATIONS

A much rarer type is the parabolic consolidation. However, although rare, this consolidation is very powerful and generally occurs before a strong advance in price. With a parabolic consolidation, nearly the entire trend leading up to the consolidation actually becomes part of the consolidation, arching in a curve on both the bottom of the trend (the support line) and the top of the trend (the resistance line) until the two arcs finally converge very, very close to the high price for the year. Figure 13-9 is an example of this type of consolidation.

FIGURE 13-9: PARABOLIC CONSOLIDATION

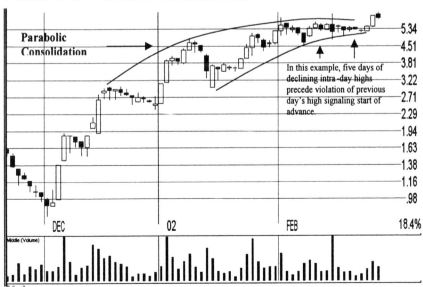

Again, there are a number of places where declining intra-day highs and then a violation of the previous day's high signal the start of the advance. You can enter the stock at any of these decline and upside violation situations with a minimum of risk, and without much concern about needing to buy only at the ultimate breakout from the consolidation. In other words, you need to pick a limited-risk entry point, but you don't need to wait until the stock has made a new high or has fully formed a base. You just need to wait until there's been a series of declining intra-day highs and then a violation. Once you buy the stock, to limit your risk, place a sell-stop under the lowest intra-day low for the previous two days.

The day-to-day price action of some stocks can be somewhat erratic, and the series of declining intra-day highs never occurs. On these stocks, you have to wait for them to rise above the line of resistance (the resistance-violation technique) on the consolidation before buying. In this case, you will again limit your risk by placing your sell-stop order under the lowest intra-day low of the past two days (see Figure 13-10).

FIGURE 13-10: RESISTANCE LINE

Figure 13-10 is an excellent example of how, when you understand the composition of stock trends, you can spot many, many limited-loss entry points in just about any advancing stock. Limited-loss entry points developed in Figure 13-10 at points A, B, C, D, and E. There may be other possible entry points, but these are the most obvious. In each case, a series of declining intra-day highs was violated on the upside, signaling an opportune time to buy with a defined potential loss and unlimited upside potential. At point A, the declines in the intra-day high were a bit erratic, so you might not have bought until the stock violated the price high of the previous two or three days. You would have immediately placed a sell-stop order at the place indicated, under the low of the previous two days (that is, the lowest of the intra-day trading price of the day you bought and of the day before you bought).

The simplest way to take advantage of these buying opportunities is to place a buy-stop order one-half to one percent above the previous day's high price. This way, you won't have to watch the market quite as closely. Always place your sell-stop immediately after buying. Always!

CONSOLIDATION COLLAPSE AND RECOVERY

You may also wish to capitalize on the phenomenon of consolidation collapse and recovery. When a sharp break occurs, taking a stock outside its consolidation range on the downside, watch to see if a recovery occurs within a day or two. If not, move on. If the price does recover into the previous limits of the consolidation, look for a series of declining highs or some other resistance level as an entry point. Often, consolidations that collapse and then recover within a day or two advance steadily from there. The reason is that the weak holders of the stock were shaken out by the rapid price decline, which has the added benefit of clearing out built-up sell-stop orders. In other words, many of the people who would otherwise be waiting to sell into any rally have already sold out their positions, leaving only strong holders and people looking to buy the stock. Hence, the advance from there is steady and fairly uninterrupted. Figure 13-11 shows a very typical example of this type of action.

After the collapse, the stock within a matter of two or three days was back within the trading range of the previously intact consolidation. At that point, you would be looking for some resistance level or a series of declining highs from which to enter the stock on upside violation of the resistance or previous day's high. The upside violation came at point A, when you would have bought your position at slightly more than $53 per share, immediately placing a sell-stop at the previous two days' low (just below A). About a week later, another two days of declining highs would have given you another chance to enter the stock at just over $53, again with limited risk of loss. Finally, if you missed those two opportunities, you could have entered the stock at point B, as the stock made a new 52-week high, placing your sell-stop below the low of the previous two days' trading.

FIGURE 13-11: CONSOLIDATION COLLAPSE AND RECOVERY

RAPID-DECLINE CONSOLIDATIONS

There is one formation that, while it can present profit opportunities, is more difficult to maneuver and can be treacherous. This is the rapid-declining consolidation. In this formation, the consolidation slopes not slightly but rapidly downward, at a rate only slightly less steep than the preceding ascent. It also erases a third or more of the preceding advance. Figure 13-12 is a very typical rapid-decline consolidation chart.

FIGURE 13-12: RAPID-DECLINE CONSOLIDAITON

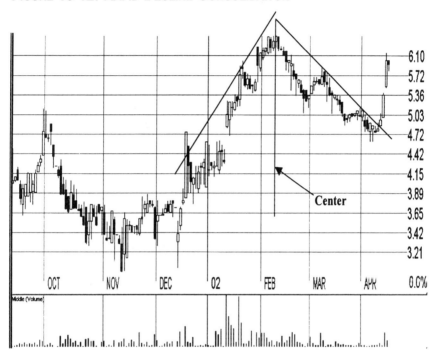

Notice that from the centerline, the angle of ascent and the angle of descent are only *slightly* different. This is what distinguishes the rapid-decline from the downward-sloping consolidation.

Rapid-decline consolidations can be a precedent to higher prices, but I don't recommend trading them, because they're difficult to play profitably. Because the rate of descent is so rapid, it can be hard to differentiate between a rapid-decline consolidation and a plain old downtrend. There are better entry opportunities that are more reliable.

ELEPHANT-HUNTING

When you buy a stock, you're naturally looking for a large increase. As an investor, you should have no interest in buying stocks with only a 20 percent appreciation potential. You want the large percentage gain that comes from long-term holding, not a series of 20 percent profits that fill your days with rapid-fire trading and other busywork. That means that in the stock market, you have to be an elephant-hunter.

Elephant-hunters don't let the rabbits distract them. They look for stocks that can mount substantial increases in price over a long period. That's why it makes sense to periodically review long-term charts—and to know what to look for.

Here is one way to find stocks that have higher potential for a long-term gain. First, look for stocks that have had a good percentage rise over the past five years. You should be looking at these stock charts where each bar represents between five to 10 trading days per bar. (TeleChart 2000 makes it very easy to find the stocks that have good five-year growth rates, and also makes it easy to view the long-term chart.)

Look for stocks showing consolidations (flat-top, declining, or parabolic) that are as much as one or two years long. These are the stocks that may have been toying with the new-highs list for a long time (in the case of a flat-top consolidation), and have been building strength all the while. A stock emerging from a one-year consolidation has a better chance to advance over the long-term than one emerging from a two-month consolidation. The longer the consolidation, the greater the potential percentage increases. You want to get in on the upward move as early as possible after a stock emerges from such a consolidation. Figures 13-13 and 13-14 are examples of stocks showing this type of chart pattern.

In Figure 13-13, the stock has already broken out of its consolidation and appears poised for a potentially large increase in price, continuing its excellent trend of several years before. Volume has risen as it has emerged from the consolidation, indicating muscle behind the move. To enter this stock, you could wait for a precision entry point using the descending highs technique, or you could simply buy into your position, placing a sell-stop at 70 (below the previous line of resistance) to protect yourself from a meltdown.

You're probably thinking that placing a sell-stop at 70 when the stock is at 86.50 could result in a huge percentage loss. True, but when you're taking long-term positions, you don't need to be overly concerned about adhering to anyone's one-size fits-all stop-loss parameters (e.g., "never take more than an 8 percent loss"); nor do you need to adhere to dictums about not buying beyond a certain percentage above the resistance line, etc. These ideas will only keep you from getting into stocks that are showing a lot of promise.

FIGURE 13-13: MULTI-YEAR FLAT-TOP CONSOLIDATION

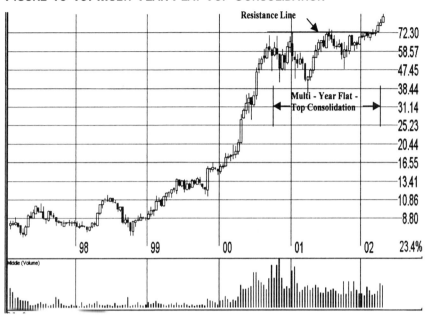

FIGURE 13-14: MULTI-YEAR DECLINING CONSOLIDATION

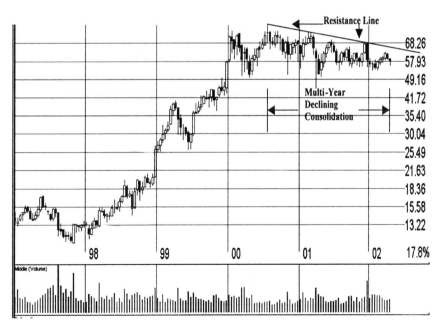

What you do need to do is to size your position so that, if the worst happens with this particular stock, you won't exceed your drawdown parameters as a percent of your account value. For instance, say you had the following situation:

Account value: $100,000
Targeted drawdown: One percent
   (You will risk no more than one percent of your account value
   on any one trade.)
Sell-stop position: $70 per share
Current stock price: $86.50 per share

You would calculate how much stock to buy as follows:

$100,000 x .01 (1% maximum loss per trade) = $1,000 maximum risk
$86.50 - $70.00 = $16.50 (difference between current price and stock price)
$1,000 (maximum loss) ÷ $16.50 per share = 61 shares

You decide to buy 61 shares of the stock at a cost of about $5,276. If you had either a larger drawdown parameter or decided to risk being stopped out prematurely by setting your stop order closer, you would have bought more. Of course, if with the Reverse Scale System you have every other initial position at $5,000, you'd want to be consistent, and so you would buy 57 shares.

In Figure 13-14, the stock has not yet emerged from the consolidation phase and it cannot be assumed that it will, so the successful investor goes on watch, patiently waiting to see if the stock emerges above the line of resistance and buying only then. When playing these long-term consolidations, you need to give the stocks some allowance—at least 10 percent—for volatility as they are rising above the line of resistance. Otherwise you may get stopped out of your position even if the stock is in the process of going higher.

OTHER CONSIDERATIONS FOR ELEPHANT-HUNTING

Obviously, stocks that have elephant-potential consolidations still need to meet our other criteria—they should not be defensive issues, sales growth should be positive, and so on. As always, they will only work when bullish conditions prevail, so keep Trading Rule Four in mind at all times.

CHAPTER SUMMARY

Periodically scan the long-term charts of five-year gainers for elephant-potential consolidations. Keep a list of promising candidates to watch. If you watch them diligently, you can be sure of being there when the stock rises above the resistance point, hopefully resulting in a multi-year, many fold increase in price.

CONCLUSION

At this point, you have all the tools, rules, concepts, and techniques you need to have success, even great success, in the stock market. How much success you have will be determined by only two things (1) market conditions and (2) your ability to control your own actions. While nothing can be done about market conditions, your actions are the one critical component that you can control.

There can be, and will be, long periods of time when you should do nothing, according to the rules in this book. You may need to stay largely in cash when Trading Rule Four says that it's a bear market, or you may simply have to hold current positions without adding to or liquidating them when the markets are in the doldrums. For many people, these are the hardest times, especially for those who are action-oriented. Yet, to take action when the rules say not to will only diminish your returns in the long-run.

For other personality types, the times that require action may be the hardest. Some persons are deliberate in nature; they have difficulty with quick decisions and quick action. Yet there are times when these also are required.

Let the rules I've presented alone determine when it's time for quick action and when it's time for no action. Follow them. Analyze yourself just enough to understand whether you're the deliberate type or the impulsive, action-oriented type. Try to correct those tendencies so you can follow the logical rules in the Reverse Scale System. If you do, you will have far less stress. More important, over time you will achieve far greater profits.

INDEX

W

Walt Disney, 8
Wiest, Robert F., 124

X

Xerox, 8

Y

Yahoo! Finance, 26, 78, 99,104, 112,
114, 115
Yield curve diversion, 169
You Can't Lose Trading Commodities,
122
Your Battle for Stock Market Profits, 66